ABANDONED & BETRAYED BY GOD

ALSO BY REV. DR. JIM STOUT

All books are (or soon will be) available online through Amazon and other stores in both printed and e-book formats. Further information can be found by visiting Dr. Stout's website, www.drjimstout.com.

Please consider purchasing some of these life-enhancing publications for yourself, or as gifts for family members, friends, patients, clergy, or mental-medical health providers. They are ideal for encouragement gifts, bulk orders, special promotions, and other uses. A portion of the profits from these will be used for various mental illness, clergy, and career-guidance ministries.

BIPOLAR DISORDER—REBUILDING YOUR LIFE:
A Bipolar's Story That Includes Practical Strategies, Techniques, and Tips for Managing Moods

RECOVERING AND REBUILDING FROM A SEVERE MENTAL ILLNESS:
A Personal Story of Faith and Mental Illness

BOUNDARY SETTING:
A Practical Guide

BOUNDARY SETTING FOR CLERGY AND MINISTRY WORKERS:
A Practical Guide to Protecting Your Ministry and Minimizing Stress

MENTAL ILLNESS AND YOUR MARRIAGE:
Strategies for Repairing and Enriching Your Marriage

CRUSHED DREAMS:
How to Overcome Unmet Expectations

STRESS BUSTING:
User-Friendly Approaches for Coping with Stress-Causing People and Situations

BEATING DEPRESSION:
Practical Techniques to Survive, Cope, Heal, and Rebuild

WRITINGS OF PAIN, WRITINGS OF HOPE:
A Candid Glimpse into the Thinking of a Suicidally-Depressed Christian Leader

CHANGING GEARS:
Making the Most of the Second Half of Your Life

THE EMERGENCY GUIDE TO DEPRESSION AND BIPOLAR:
How to Survive a Crisis

TIME TO REBOUND:
How to Find Your Purpose in Life Despite Your Losses

BUILDING A STRONGER MARRIAGE AND FAMILY:
A Helpful Guide to Mending and Enhancing Your Home Life

ABANDONED & BETRAYED BY GOD

SURVIVING A CRISIS OF FAITH

REV. DR. JIM STOUT

SHEPHERD PUBLISHING

The information in this book is intended to complement, not substitute for, the advice of your physician, psychiatrist, psychologist, MFT, MSW, or other mental-medical health provider. Please consult him or her about your unique needs. If you are in urgent difficulty, phone 911 or a crisis hotline, such as the National Suicide Prevention Crisis Hotline at 1-800-273-TALK (1-800-273-8255).

Edited by Andrew Kroeger and Stephanie Starr. Cover design by Andrew Kroeger.

Cover photo from iStock.

ISBN: 978-1-942648-02-4

DEDICATED WITH GRATITUDE

To Leah, my awesome wife of nearly fifty years, who has tried her best to understand my circumstances and patiently accept my reactions to them. Her unconditional support and nonstop prayers have kept me going. Her love has inspired me to overcome obstacle after obstacle and finish this book.

To my close friends and contemporaries who have already trudged the desolate roads of spiritual crises. Their life-sustaining words of guidance and empathy have been an awesome gift.

To my friends who, by God's grace, have *not* had to walk the dark path themselves, yet stood by me, keeping me afloat by their prayers, nonjudgmental listening, and sensitive words of encouragement.

To the countless Christian brothers and sisters who suffered through bleak periods in their lives, enduring faith trials with a tenacious trust that somehow God was with them in their pain and would see them through. They blazed a trail for me by teaching not only life-saving lessons of faith survival but also positive living strategies.

To those people who have now entered into the unsurpassed joys of heaven, and have left behind written records of their struggles and victories.

AUTHOR'S NOTES

For the reader's convenience, and for clarification, I have:

- used the *New International Version* for all Bible verses, added reference endnotes with verse location, and italicized all verses;
- used either *he* or *she* rather than the longer *he and/or she* for brevity when referring to men or women. In most cases, *he* or *she* is intended to refer to anyone, regardless of gender; and
- changed certain names in order to protect an individual's privacy.

Faith, like a jackal, feeds among the tombs, and even from these dead doubts she gathers her most vital hope.

Herman Melville, Moby-Dick

CONTENTS

PREFACE

*What do we live for if it is not to make life
less difficult for each other?*

George Eliot

DAY AFTER DAY, I SLOGGED THROUGH ANGRY FRUSTRATION OVER my derailed plans. I somberly wondered, "Why weren't my prayers answered? Why hasn't God comforted me in my losses? Why did he lead me this way, providing one confirmation after another, only to pull the rug out from under me?"

At first, I hesitated to discuss my deep, inner feelings with anyone, let alone write about them, lest my words hinder another believer's faith. When I finally gained the courage to share my faith battles, the first two Christians I approached outright shamed me, saying, "Jim, you shouldn't think that way. You have a strong faith. Act on it."

I realize that by grappling with God's apparent absence and betrayal, and by voicing my own upsets, I'm risking that my words may cause some to lose their faith. However, I'm compelled to mention my own inner wars, and those of others, to reassure you and other faith-wrestlers that you are not alone—you have lots of company, and there is a way through your despair.

THIS BOOK IS FOR PEOPLE GOING THROUGH SPIRITUAL PAIN

Are you going through a difficult loss? Are your emotions shredded by a loved one's death, an ended relationship, a terminated job, a failed important project, or a soured dream?

Are you missing God's comfort, reassurance, and presence? Does it seem like he has deserted you? When you experience such distress and don't get any peace from God or his Scriptures, the pain and loneliness can be almost too much to bear.

Do you feel that God has let you down? misled you? tricked you? even betrayed you? When you've done your best to obediently walk through each of the doors he's opened for you and then an important one slams in your face, it really hurts. And it scalds you with anger and the bitter feeling that you've been set up, even deceived.

Or do you think God has both abandoned *and* betrayed you? You demand, "Why has God allowed or even caused all this to happen? Why hasn't he made things clearer? Why hasn't he intervened? Where's the inner peace he pledged? Why won't he answer my prayers?"

Can you identify with these experiences? If you can, then welcome to the Crisis-of-Faith Misery Club. You've got lots of company—countless Christians have suffered through faith upheavals and grappled with similar feelings of abandonment and betrayal. I've written this book because, as tough as things may be for you, I believe you can get through it.

THE WRITING PROCESS

For me, one of the most helpful ways to process inner hurts has been to write down my thoughts and feelings. I've written these pages during bleak days and miserable nights, often into the wee hours of the morning. I've jotted things down in my car, in restaurants, in my office, in church, and while sitting in my family room's reclining chair. I've written on napkins, scraps of paper, hotel notepads, even magazine covers.

This free-flowing exercise often gave me a strange sort of cathartic release and injected a different outlook on my situation. For several months, I wrote randomly about my experiences of feeling spiritually abandoned and betrayed by God, thinking no one else would see it. But then I realized others might benefit from reading my thoughts, and I organized my notes into an essay, which eventually evolved into this book.

These words have passed through a grid of hurts, raw doubts, hard-nosed questions, ongoing examinations of the Scriptures, and voracious reading of the writings of other Christian strugglers. This book is a result of the good, the bad, and the ugly experiences I had from living for many months in spiritual limbo. It also shares my prayers for help, insight, and direction.

Although at times I felt like I was receiving no reassurance or guidance from God, the process of writing this book has improved my understanding of him and his mysterious ways. It has strengthened my reliance on his genuine care for me, as well as his redirection of my faltering steps.

In addition to these personal writings, I have added the things I've learned from interviews and counseling sessions with hundreds of Christian clergy and laypersons throughout the past forty-five years. I've also included the wisdom from writings of past and contemporary Christ followers, many who have gone through far worse faith-testing than I have.

MY GOALS IN WRITING THIS BOOK

The purpose of *Abandoned and Betrayed by God* is to describe the inner battles I've fought during spiritually-empty periods and to offer practical support in weathering these storms.

To achieve these goals, I have divided this book into two parts:

- **Part One: Experiencing a Crisis of Faith** describes the lonely experiences of me and others who have journeyed into the black pit of a faith crisis. I share my personal story, including the lessons I have learned and the benefits that have come from my spiritual battles.
- **Part Two: Guidelines for Surviving a Crisis of Faith** is a practical resource of suggested steps to process your own faith darkness and then rebuild a new, deeper faith.

I'm inspired by the writer of Proverbs, who said, *"I applied my heart to what I observed and learned a lesson from what I saw."* [1] These pages represent my own take on processing spiritual desolation. I share this so that those with dimmed faith might find hope and encouragement in their faith crises. It is my strong hope that, having overcome their struggles, my readers will be better equipped to share their own strength and experience with those who are still struggling.

I realize that the particular recovery methods found in this book may not be of benefit in your unique situation. But please try to keep an open mind and be willing to experiment with new ways of dealing with your spiritual crisis. I certainly honor your choices and I respect your results, be they a forever-lost faith or a renewed one.

INTRODUCTION

Alas, how easily things go wrong!
A sigh too much or a kiss too long,
And there follows a mist or a weeping rain,
And life is never the same again.

George MacDonald, Phantastes

IN THE 1500S, ST. JOHN OF THE CROSS FIRST USED THE PHRASE "DARK NIGHT of the soul" to describe his sense of deep spiritual despair. Since then, countless Christians have slogged through similar soul-numbing periods that are lonely beyond words. The entire issue of *Leadership Journal's* Fall 2011 edition focused on this phenomenon of terrible spiritual void:

> As we researched this issue of *Leadership Journal*, we quickly learned that many if not most church leaders readily admit to having experienced a dark night of the soul . . . As painful and disorienting as these times may be, it's in the darkness that God does some of his best work. [1]

This raw experience can rock a person's faith, and the hard reality is that some do not survive it—their pain and losses are too immense. For those who endure, their faith's survival requires finding their own path out of the thick fog of doubt, skepticism, guilt, fear, and isolation.

Can you identify with these feelings? If so, perhaps you can understand the following real-life examples of the men and women who felt hurt, confused, and resentful at the way God treated them.

Sarah, an unhappy married woman, sobbed:

> I prayed to God for years to lead me to the right man to marry. I truly believe he brought my husband and me together, and we enjoyed sixteen years of marriage and had three children. Suddenly, last week, he left me and our kids for his secretary. How could God have provided so much evidence that we should be married? I feel betrayed, not only by my husband but also by God.

Mike, a pastor, lamented:

> My wife and I had prayed for God to give us clear leading if we were to leave our present church and go to another. Time after time, doors opened and signs pointed to a church in the Southwest. After several visits and many discussions, its pulpit committee told me I was their unanimous choice to be their next pastor. They wanted me to start in three months and urged me to fly there in two weeks with my wife to look for a house to buy.
>
> That was six months ago. We never heard from them again. How could they be so deceitful after that upbeat meeting and the promised position? Why didn't God spare us from getting our hopes up? Why did he put us through all those seemingly positive visits? We feel tricked, deceived.

Maggie, a sexually-abused, disillusioned young woman, cried:

> I was so happy that the Lord had directed me to such a warm, accepting church and caring pastor. But, six months later, the

initial friendliness of the church members cooled. Everyone suddenly seemed aloof. I don't think I said or did anything offensive, why was I treated this way?

I shared my hurt feelings with the pastor on three occasions. On the third counseling session, he tried to molest me. Now I feel like a religious orphan—rejected by my church and exploited by its pastor. Why did God make it so clear that I was to join this church? Why won't God show me why he guided me here? Why don't I sense his closeness anymore? Is he punishing me? Now my trust in him and his followers is gone. I want nothing to do with God or church people.

Daniel and Michelle, a despairing couple, teared up as they shared their heartache:

We both wanted children so much. But due to physical problems we weren't able to conceive. So we prayed and prayed about adopting. We interviewed lots of people and agencies, filled out dozens of forms, and kept asking God to lead us to the children we were to adopt.

All the signs seemed to show that God had directed us to a particular Christian adoption agency and two specific boys: a toddler and an infant. So we jumped through all the legal hoops, filled out more forms, and, eighteen years ago, adopted our two sons.

Within a year of adopting, we started having serious problems with both boys. Over the last twenty years, we've spent thousands of dollars on psychologists, doctors, and special schools to help with their emotional problems. Yet nothing's worked. Our sons have caused us endless distress through drug and alcohol addictions, lost jobs, and other issues. Both have rejected us and our values. We're heartbroken and angry. Why did God let all this happen? Maybe God's just some kind of sadist. Or maybe he doesn't exist after all.

Can you relate to these people? Countless Christians have endured similar gut-wrenching losses. Some have kept their faith intact, others have permanently jettisoned their beliefs.

Are you processing a major disappointment right now? Please know that there's hope—others have made it through the lonely darkness of a faith meltdown, and you can too. Please hang on and keep reading.

PART ONE
EXPERIENCING A CRISIS OF FAITH

Doubts are more cruel than the worst of truths.

Jean Baptiste Moliere,

Le Misanthrope: Act III

INTRODUCTION

A SOLAR ECLIPSE OCCURS WHEN THE MOON COMPLETELY BLOTS OUT THE light of the sun. Similarly, a faith eclipse occurs when something seems to block out all hope and causes your faith in God to be weakened, even smothered.

A tragedy is rarely accompanied by God's comforting presence or a reassuring sense of his purpose for our loss. Sometimes you can see in your rearview mirror a glimpse of God's purposes in your suffering, but oftentimes you can only see darkness.

Religious doubts affect us in every way: emotionally, physically, mentally, and, of course, spiritually. The destruction of your once-strong faith unravels your comfortable concepts about God and life, as well as your understanding of what a Christian's experience should be like. This trauma undermines your self-confidence, relationships, and life priorities. It leaves collateral damage such as frayed emotions, broken friendships, and wounded self-esteem.

If this sounds familiar, take courage—you are not alone. Others have made it through the dark days and lonely nights of a collapsed relationship with God.

At this point, all talk about restoring faith may sound like empty optimism that is stuffed with theological dribble. I know—I've been there. I stewed for months in raw emotional pain, living with jaded skepticism. And so have countless other believers. Your faith restoration will take time, and it may mean enduring more suffering, but if I could survive it, you can too. And like me, someday you may even see some benefits come out of your experience.

CHAPTER 1
AN HONEST LOOK AT CHRISTIAN LIFE

My God, my God, why have you forsaken me?

Jesus Christ, from the cross,

Matthew 27:46

LIFE CAN BE SO UNSETTLING—IN ONE MOMENT, YOU MIGHT BE STANDING on top of the world, feeling totally in control of your life, and in the blink of an eye, you're watching helplessly as the world smashes you and all your carefully-laid plans into tiny pieces.

A faith crisis can be caused by a single, unexpected, disastrous event, or by multiple lesser ones. It can be caused by a prolonged illness, or several short ones. It can even be caused by recurring financial, relationship, or work problems. The list is endless.

These tough times can be horrifically lonely if you can't find solace from God's presence. And if you also feel like he's misled you, the pain of betrayal hurts even more.

A MAJOR MISCONCEPTION ABOUT CHRISTIAN LIFE

Does a successful Christian life consist of continuous well-being and joy? Is it wrong to question God or get intensely angry with him?

Plenty of Christian pastors and laypersons steadfastly believe that so long as they are walking in faithful obedience, it's not God's will that any of his children would suffer. These Christians are convinced they've developed a "spiritual success" formula for their lives that's Bible-supported and guarantees them success and happiness: "Trust and obey, then all will go well for us."

Along with King Hezekiah, each one naively thinks, *"There will be peace and security in my lifetime."* [1] These misinformed church people are resolutely wedded to the concept that the Christian life is one of victory, joy, good health, and financial prosperity—that their happiness will be ensured by praying, obeying God, and reading the Bible.

Untold numbers of Christ-followers believe that if a believer undergoes illness, economic downturn, a failed religious project, or a severe depression, it's a manifestation of some kind of religious disobedience. And that if this believer questions God's ways, or vents anger toward him, many will chalk it up to a lack of faith. These judgmental Christians accuse other faith-plagued believers with the guilt trip, "You've messed up, or none of this stuff would be happening to you."

The bottom line is that we live in a broken world, where sin and pain taints every person and every situation, regardless of a person's spirituality or religious zeal.

UNDERSTANDING THE REALITY OF LIFE'S UNFAIRNESS

Why do some people face more misfortunes than others? Some of us seem to be broadsided by one bad thing after another, while others seem to only encounter minor speed bumps.

But, sooner or later, everyone suffers in some way. Psychiatrist Scott Peck's book *The Road Less Traveled* opens with the stark phrase, "Life is difficult." The harsh fact of life is that heartache and setbacks happen. Being a nice person or a devout Christian doesn't insulate a person from pain. Fine, loving people face awful situations just as often as mean ones do. Letdowns, failures, catastrophes, tragedies, and betrayals are part of life.

No matter what its form, suffering plays no favorites. Jesus never sugarcoated the reality of life's unjustness. He explained that God *"causes his sun to rise on the evil and the good, and sends rain on the righteous and the unrighteous."* [2]

It's probably easy for you, as it is for me, to *intellectually* accept the spiritual realities of unjust suffering as something beyond our comprehension. We can agree with God when he says, *"As the heavens are higher than the earth, so are my ways higher than your ways and my thoughts than your thoughts."* [3]

Yet when we're *in the midst* of unjust circumstances, it's hard to accept that reality. I easily identify with the Old Testament hero Job, who complained bitterly about his wrongful treatment and horrific losses: *"Even today my complaint is bitter; his hand is heavy in spite of my groaning."* [4]

In fact, several years ago, I complained to my eighty-four-year-old dietitian about my unjust circumstances. Her response was priceless: "Jim, face it, life isn't fair! The Fair is in Pomona!" (the city in Southern California that hosts the area's largest fair).

Have you come to grips with life's unfairness and, in particular, your own raw deals?

EXPERIENCING FAITH-TESTING EVENTS THAT ROCK YOUR BELIEFS

For the most part, your Christian life, like mine, may be a relatively smooth journey as you enjoy special times of closeness with God and receive obvious answers to prayers. That is, until your faith is tested by a traumatic event, or a relentless series of smaller setbacks. Anger, anxiety, and questioning then become daily companions.

When things go bad in those moments, days, months, and even years, it's rarely just *one* thing happening. It's *every* thing. During this turning point, your once-steady, predictable spot in God's universe can suddenly feel like you're in the pilot seat of a fighter jet, shot down and spiraling toward the ground for a fiery crash.

My own spiritual crisis hit me hard. Moses's troubled words to God haunted me: *"Why have you brought this trouble on your servant?"* [5] Oh, how I recognized the psalmist's words of misery: *"You are God my stronghold. Why have you rejected me?"* [6]

Poor Job articulated my darker thoughts: *"Yet when I hoped for good, evil came; when I looked for light, then came darkness. The churning inside me never stops; days of suffering confront me."* [7]

Perhaps you, like Job and I, feel cornered, scared, betrayed, uncertain of what you did wrong to deserve this, and unsure of what will happen next. Maybe you are simply confused about how to regain your sense of God's reassuring presence or his intervention in your life.

In *Words of Endurance*, an online devotional, former major league baseball pitcher Dave Dravecky wrote, "When we are overwhelmed by pain—when our circumstances scream, 'This makes no sense!'—we want relief. If we can't escape the pain, we at least want some kind of explanation. When we have to endure what seems the unendurable, we want the comfort of knowing that God sees clearly and still holds our future in his able hands."

During this gloom-filled emptiness, it may feel as if everything you know about God and life is up for grabs. There's a devastating confusion of meaning and purpose, and a lack of any kind of divine consolation in your situation. At a time when you most need God's soothing nearness and guidance, all evidence points to his absence, his silence. All of the Bible's promises seem insincere, meaningless, false, and even mocking.

Maybe you feel like you've lost all hope. Dr. Lewis Smedes, a Fuller Theological Seminary professor, writes in his tender, uplifting book *Keeping Hope Alive*, "Hope can be struck by lightning, but it can also die from repeated slaps of disappointment. Hope hangs on too long sometimes, gets too tired to go on, and has nothing to do but collapse from relentless letdown." [8]

Enduring one disappointment after another, and experiencing too many shattered hopes, can devastate your faith. You can find yourself questioning the whole meaning of life and what you believed about God's character, even his existence.

Indeed, I've met quite a number of men and women who've faced such unbearable life tragedies; such unrelenting, undeserving pain; and such hypocrisy in churches that they've lost all confidence in God's existence.

William Lobdell, a once-dedicated Christian, was a religion reporter for the *Los Angeles Times* newspaper. As an on-fire believer, he specifically asked for the job of covering religious activities. For several years, he covered all sorts of events that revolved around his Christian faith.

But, during this time, Lobdell observed so much religious fraud, sexual misconduct among clergy, and unexplainable life tragedies that it finally eroded his own faith. His July 7, 2007, *Los Angeles Times* article "Religion Beat Became a Test of Faith" chronicled his "spiritual journey from devout Christian to reluctant atheist."

The article generated thousands of emails, letters, and calls. It hit a sensitive nerve, probably because there is such reluctance by religious people to talk openly and honestly about their doubts, about why a loving God could permit such heartaches as immoral or unethical clergy, religious leaders who were active pedophiles, poverty, cancer, and wars.

I certainly admire Lobdell's courageous integrity and I resonate with his struggling. Can you relate to his experiences?

CHRISTIAN SUFFERING CAN MAKE YOU FEEL ABANDONED AND BETRAYED BY GOD

A faith catastrophe is often triggered by an overwhelming sense of God's abandonment or betrayal. In order to avoid any misunderstandings, let's see how *Webster's New World College Dictionary* defines two key words:

> **Abandon**: To give up (something) completely or forever; to leave; forsake; desert
>
> **Betray**: To hand over; to break faith with; fail to meet the hopes of; to lead astray [9]

To feel abandoned by God is to sense that you're absolutely cut off from him, with no divine intervention, no comforting presence. You get no soothing reassurance from normal spiritual sources like prayer, Bible reading, or fellowship with other believers. It's a time of utter solitude in the universe.

Many Christians, including myself, lean on God's assurance: *"Never will I leave you; never will I forsake you."* [10] For many devout people, just the suggestion that God might leave us is offensive. To some believers, the thought of God's total absence from their life is a painful, unspeakable notion. Yet, over forty times, the Scriptures mention God's seeming unavailability, and it encourages us to wait for him until he returns.

As bad as it is to feel abandoned, the sense that God has betrayed you is even worse. Betrayal is a breach of trust—it includes acts of lying, deceiving, double-crossing, cheating, gossiping, undermining, stealing, and other actions.

A lot of Christians experience frequent validation that they are doing the right thing, taking obedient steps of faith. Then, as they are trying to follow what they believe is God's unmistakable guidance, their aspirations collapse. They are shocked, disillusioned! It seems to them that God has pulled the rug out from under their feet, that they've been strung along under deceitful reassurances, false pretenses. They sense that God has not only left them, but also set them up for failure.

Feeling abandoned and betrayed by God is a living hell. God appears to be indifferent, remote, and cruel. It's a helpless, pain-filled, fearful, and angry existence that often spirals into despair. You are left with no explanations of God's purposes, no awareness of his presence, and no affirmation, support, or guidance from him. Your faith is crushed, and you feel as though you are left totally alone to fend for yourself in a haphazard, callous, unforgiving world.

BIBLE HEROES WHO FELT ABANDONED OR BETRAYED BY GOD

When you're going through the agonizing loneliness of a faith meltdown, it's strangely comforting to know that others have gone through similar experiences. Many Bible heroes endured—and overcame—lengthy faith collapses.

King David writhed with a sense of God's abandonment, and David's words often reflected his mixed feelings about God.

At one spiritual high point, David wrote, *"God is our refuge and strength, an ever-present help in trouble"* [11] and, *"Where can I go from your Spirit? Where can I flee from your presence? If I go up to the heavens, you are there; if I make my bed in the depths, you are there."* [12]

Yet even after writing those strong words of faith, there were times when he was absolutely convinced God had abandoned him. David lamented God's silence: *"My God, my God, why have you forsaken me? Why are you so far from saving me, so far from my cries of anguish?"* [13] And he wondered, *"How long, O Lord? Will you forget me forever? How long will you hide your face from me? How long must I wrestle with my thoughts and every day have sorrow in my heart? . . . Return to us, O God Almighty!"* [14]

Job also ached when he felt deserted and deceived by God. As strong as Job's faith was, when he suffered loss after loss, he yelled out to God: *"Why do you hide your face and consider me your enemy?"* [15]

Having lost everything dear to him, Job bemoaned: *"Therefore I will not keep silent; I will speak out of the anguish of my spirit, I will complain in the bitterness of my soul."* [16] He lamented, *"As water wears away stones and torrents wash away the soil, so you destroy a man's hope."* [17]

Job persistently complained about his treatment by God: *"He has blocked my way so I cannot pass; he has shrouded my paths in darkness . . . He tears me down on every side till I am gone; he uproots my hope like a tree. His anger burns against me; he counts me among his enemies."* [18]

Similarly, the prophet Jeremiah cried out, *"You deceived me, Lord, and I was deceived."* [19] He lamented God's betrayal:

He has driven me away and made me walk in darkness rather than light. Indeed, he has turned his hand against me again and again, all day long . . . He has besieged me and surrounded me with bitterness and hardship . . . Even when I call out or cry for

help, he shuts out my prayer . . . I have been deprived of peace . . .
My splendor is gone and all that I had hoped for from the Lord. [20]

You may relate to the cries of Gideon: *"If the Lord is with us, why has all this happened to us? Where are all his wonders that our ancestors told us about? . . . But now the Lord has abandoned us."* [21]

The Old Testament widow Naomi felt betrayed by God. She groaned, *"Don't call me Naomi [pleasant]; call me Mara [bitter], because the Almighty has made my life very bitter."* [22]

Even our Savior, Jesus, knew the brutal loneliness of being abandoned by his Father when he cried out from the cross, *"My God, my God, why have you forsaken me?"* [23] Jesus also knew what it was like to feel betrayed, telling his disciples, *"The Son of Man is going to be delivered into the hands of men."* [24]

POINTS TO PONDER:

- Do you ever feel that life has dealt you a raw deal—or far too many?
- How has your understanding of the Christian life been affected by life's unfairness?
- Can you identify with people who've felt a sense of abandonment or betrayal by God?

SUGGESTED ACTION STEP:

Write a paragraph or two about your abandonment-betrayal battle, describing what happened and how you feel about it.

CHAPTER 2
MY OWN CRISIS OF FAITH

My spirit is broken . . . my days have
passed, my plans are shattered.

Job 17:1, 11

AS A CHILD, I LOVED PLAYING ON THE TEETER-TOTTER AT OUR LOCAL park. A friend would sit on one end of the board and I'd sit on the other, and we'd bounce each other up and down. Sometimes when I was the one who was down, I would stay there, leaving my friend stuck up in the air, screaming to be let down. Then I'd pull a mean trick: while he was still in the air, I'd jump off the teeter-totter and he'd crash to the ground.

There have been times when I felt God has done that to me. I looked to him to be with me through the ups and downs of life, but when a plan, project, or relationship fell apart, it felt like he had cruelly left me hanging just so he could watch me fall.

WHAT TRIGGERED MY FAITH CRISIS?

In my lifetime, I've fought through several major spiritual battles, but the torments of a faith ordeal in 2007 shook me to the core. That year,

I firmly believed God had directed me to several great opportunities, but the most important one was writing and publishing a second book on bipolar disorder.

At first, several important doors were opened: I'd obtained a gifted literary agent, my coauthor psychiatrist eagerly agreed to write two chapters, and a well-known publisher offered us a contract that included a nice signing bonus.

I was excited and fully committed to my book project. I spent several hundred hours researching books and periodicals. I scoured the Internet for the latest information, and I interviewed individuals, family members, and mental health professionals.

Not only had I done my research, I'd also covered the more practical bases: I'd bought more than $5,000 of office equipment, including a new computer, printer, and other gear, as well as purchased relevant books, magazines, and journals.

I discussed the project with dozens of experts. All feedback was positive. To my mind, all lights were green.

In the beginning, my well-prayed-for, well-prepared plans went smoothly. I consulted almost daily with God, the Bible, and friends. Every step of the way, it seemed God had affirmed the details of my efforts. This opportunity seemed like a spiritual slam dunk.

Then my dreams for fun and success suddenly disintegrated. Six months into dealing with my senior editor, the publishing speed bumps became too frequent to ignore, too stressful to handle. With chapter deadlines to meet, I needed quick feedback to proceed, and my editor didn't respond to emails and phone calls for weeks at a time.

The final straw was when we finally connected and the editor insisted that I change a significant part of the book. My heart sank, my knees buckled, and my stomach retched. I agonized, "This change is contrary to the original proposal and undermines my vision for the book. If the editor is making a major kind of alteration this early in the game after only five chapters, how many more substantive alterations will be demanded?"

A few days later, I pulled the plug on the book venture and ended my relationship with the publishing company.

MY SPIRITUAL ANGUISH BEGINS

The collapse of the book deal hit me hard. I sank, anchored to my office chair, too stunned to move or make decisions. My body was immobilized, but my mind flew, flashing instant replays of all the undeserved hurts I was going through. I'd experienced far worse faith-shredding obstacles over the years, but for some reason, this latest one really got to me, ripping open old, inner gashes. Inwardly, I screamed:

God, I thought you wanted me to undertake this project for you. Did I misread my circumstances as signs from you? Why did you take me this far only to totally shut me down? I've invested so much time, money, and energy on this opportunity. Why, after so many opened doors, when I was so close to finishing your task, did you pull the plug on me? Why have you withdrawn your comforting peace, God? Where's your consoling presence, your guidance, now, Lord?

But no miraculous changes came my way. God sent no warm affirmations of any kind to assure me of his presence. Feeling helpless, I shouted at him:

How could you have let all these terrible things happen? Why haven't you stepped in to change things and rescue me? Have I just imagined that you've been leading me into these situations? Have I been misunderstanding *my* wishes for being *your* will? Are you punishing me? God, if you are really here, if you care, please help me rebuild and go on.

SPIRITUAL ABANDONMENT

All my prayers to God for help and guidance were met with utter silence. As a result, my inward hell stretched way beyond its initial jolt and continued relentlessly.

For two years after the book deal, my life seemed to be made up of senseless letdowns, totally without any sign of God's presence, purpose, or caring.

All signs led me to believe that God had left me, and I felt like the Israelite living in Babylonian captivity who complained: *"My way is hidden from the Lord; my cause is disregarded by my God."* [1]

I'd caught a closer glimpse of what the prophet Isaiah must have felt when he braced himself in the midst of God's hiddenness, groaning, *"Truly you are a God who has been hiding himself."* [2] And I can relate to the pain he felt when, in an even deeper state of despair, he thought to himself, *"The Lord has forsaken me, the Lord has forgotten me."* [3]

I was fully convinced that God had permanently walked out on me, leaving me to wander alone in complete darkness. Having lost the awareness of his soothing presence, and left alone without any direction to survive, my mental battles were almost unbearable. These invisible, internal wounds gnawed at me day and night. In my confusion, I moaned:

How long will this exile from God last? Why is God so silent? Why won't he show himself? Why can't he at least give me an explanation for all these recent painful events? Why can't he give me even a small sign that will let me know he's still on my side, that he still cares for me, that all these terrible things will somehow turn out for my good and his glory?

In his book *A Grief Observed,* C. S. Lewis wrote about his wife's death from cancer, describing the awfulness of God's absence:

Meanwhile, where is God? This is one of the most disquieting symptoms. When you are happy, so happy that you have no sense of needing him, if you turn to him with praise, you will be welcomed with open arms. But go to him when your need is desperate, when all other help is in vain, and what do you find? A door slammed in your face and a sound of bolting and double bolting on the inside. After that, silence. You may as well turn away. The longer you wait, the more emphatic the silence will become. [4]

Oh, how I craved for God to say to me what he said to the prophet Isaiah:

For a brief moment I abandoned you, but with deep compassion I will bring you back. In a surge of anger I hid my face from you for a moment, but with everlasting kindness I will have compassion on you . . . though the mountains be shaken and the hills be removed, yet my unfailing love for you will not be shaken nor my covenant of peace be removed. [5]

The prophet Jeremiah, speaking on behalf of God, promised to the Jewish exiles abandoned in Babylonia, *"You will seek me and find me when you seek me with all your heart. I will be found by you."* [7] Time after time, I pleaded, demanded, even begged, for God to come back, to reveal himself to me. But he seemed to pay no attention to my plight—no divine intervention, no rescue.

It was as though he'd left me treading water on an ink-black night, unable to see land and too tired to continue swimming. All I could do was keep repeating my hollow-sounding prayers for help, and hope that he'd return to me an awareness of his personal guidance in my life.

A BETRAYAL THAT STINGS

As bad as God's abandonment felt, the belief that I'd been betrayed by God hurt *far worse*. His apparent duplicity stung my mind, numbed my soul, and frayed my emotions. Just beneath the surface of my normally calm, jovial persona, I bubbled with anger, distress, confusion, cynicism, guilt, and self-questioning. I was like a boiling cauldron ready to erupt. I agonized:

Were all those open doors just smoke-and-mirror ploys by God? Was he deliberately seducing me by opening all them just to trick me by locking this last major one? Maybe all the openings I walked through weren't really God-opened doors after all. Perhaps my own agenda, my own wishes, forced doors to open that God had really closed.

Inwardly, I railed:

God, why have you let so many things sour on me over the past six months? Time and again, I received what I believed were clear-cut validations from you. I've done all kinds of due diligence. I've scrutinized my decisions thoroughly. I've discussed and received positive feedback on this book project with plenty of knowledgeable people. And I checked in repeatedly with you through prayer and reading my Bible.

I was doing my best to obediently trust you. On my own, I would have given up in the face of all these problems, but I've kept fighting precisely because I believed you were not only guiding me, but also encouraging me to continue my efforts. For me, the whole book endeavor has been a step in faith, not an ego trip. All along, I've felt I've been operating under your orders. That's why your betrayal hurts so much.

In my confusion, I questioned God:

Was there some past sin in my life that disqualified me from receiving easy-to-understand signals from you? Was it your intent to punish me by providing me with a publisher, a literary agent, and a respected co-author just so you could then cruelly humiliate me with a series of troubles that finally forced me to cancel the contract?

I wondered, sometimes in silence, sometimes out loud:

Why is God so unconcerned with my well-being? One major hurt is bad enough, but so many in a row has become intolerable. All along, I've been trying to do his will. Things aren't supposed to happen this way."

I mulled over Job's complaints:

Have I not wept for those in trouble? Has not my soul grieved for the poor? Yet when I hoped for good, evil came; when I looked for light, then came darkness. The churning inside me never stops; days of suffering confront me.[8]

Indeed, God had become an acute disappointment to me. I sincerely thought I knew his will for my projects. I did my best to obey what I believed to be his guidance, but everything backfired on me. And I resented his actions—or inactions. I simmered in self-pity and rage. I thought God had strung me along and arranged my plans to fail so he could watch me fall apart.

POINTS TO PONDER:

- Does reading about my trauma trigger any memories of similar past upsets?
- Do you ever feel like God has slammed the door on you despite all your good intentions? How does it feel? What thoughts run through your mind?
- Are you being ruthlessly honest with God about your anger and hurt? Are you telling him your doubts about him and his lack of intervention in your problem?

SUGGESTED ACTION STEP:

Tell God that his silence is disturbing you. Ask him to communicate with you in some way through a person, movie, book, song, the Bible, or some other way.

CHAPTER 3
THE SPIRITUAL CONSEQUENCES OF MY CRISIS

No one is concerned for me. I have no refuge;
no one cares for my life.

Psalms 142:4

I, WHO HAD STRONGLY BELIEVED AND ENCOURAGED SCORES OF OTHERS
to cling to Bible messages such as, *"God is our refuge and strength, an
ever-present help in trouble,"* [1] now felt that God's pledge was empty.

I could try to pretend, "Everything's not so bad. Plenty of others
face far worse circumstances." Or I could force myself to believe that
these reversals were really *my* fault: "I didn't hear God's voice clearly.
I pushed my own agenda rather than his. Now I've got to suffer the
consequences of getting too far ahead of God."

All these broken expectations felt like I'd been pummeled for ten
rounds in a boxing match. I didn't know how much more I could
take. I certainly identified with the pain-seared words of Jeremiah, *"I
am worn out with groaning and find no rest"* [2] and Paul, *"I have great
sorrow and unceasing anguish in my heart."* [3]

This constant spiritual battering began to influence my understanding of God's character. This is quite common—even C. S. Lewis went through a similar experience. In *A Grief Observed*, he wrote, "Not that I am (I think) in much danger of ceasing to believe in God. The real danger is of coming to believe such dreadful things about him. The conclusion I dread is not 'So there's no God after all,' but 'So this is what God's really like.' " [4]

On quite a few desperate occasions during my spiritual isolation, my thinking wavered between hopelessness, cynicism, blaming others, and self-condemnation. I struck out at God:

> You've let me down too many times. Not only have you been silent, you've been cruel to me. I know I've not been nearly as spiritually disciplined as I could have been, but all along, I've tried to maintain a close relationship with you.
>
> Yet this year you have treated me far worse than the betrayals of some of my so-called friends. Perhaps my unfavorable circumstances have indicated that you are, in fact, just out to punish me for my past sins. Maybe I've just been deluding myself about you and your ways, even your existence.

During the heat of my faith battle, I wasn't sure why God was treating me so strangely. Was I being tested like King Hezekiah? The Bible records: *"God left [Hezekiah] to test him and to know everything that was in his heart."* [5]

At other times, I found that the Bible appeared to contradict itself. Lamentations states that God *"does not willingly bring affliction or grief to anyone,"* implying that he *doesn't* hurt his people. [6] Yet elsewhere in the Bible, it implies that sometimes God *does* treat his people in hurtful ways: *"The Spirit of the Lord had departed from Saul, and an evil spirit **from the Lord** tormented him."* [7] Statements like these troubled me: "Have I misinterpreted the Scriptures? Will God harm me in some way?"

It's hard to stick it out when your confidence in God has eroded, when you've just had your dreams snuffed out. All outward circumstances show that God has deserted you and won't help you. Your loss points to the "evidence" that God is punishing you, that there will be no supernatural rescue, no helpful explanation, no comforting words. Just deafening silence. Mentally, I wrestled with thoughts such as, "Did God *cause* my dreams to vanish, or did he simply *allow* it?"

Ultimately, I knew I needed to have faith that God was God, and that I couldn't do anything about my dimmed hopes other than rely on his loving character. I needed to believe that, somehow, he would see me through this horrible, spiritless murk.

But I was a long way from that kind of trust. I felt that God was mean spirited, toying with me and pushing me to see when I'd crack. I mulled over and over, "Why would God seem to give something to me, only to take it away?"

LOSS OF HOPE

This spiritual misery tainted my thoughts, relationships, and activities. I questioned within myself, "Now that some of my best hopes, detailed plans, and hard work have been destroyed, what is my purpose in life? What was I born for?"

I desperately wanted to come through these aching experiences better off and somehow closer to God. I yearned to restore the joy of my salvation, to experience inner peace again, and to reignite my faith-flame. But I didn't know where to begin or what to do.

As I considered what the future might bring, my questions multiplied and my fears grew. I couldn't fathom why God had allowed me to go through so many upsets: "Lord, if I launch another project and encounter dead ends, will you pull me through? Where will you be when I face another confused spiritual wilderness? Will you just leave me to my own resources to fend for myself, like you have this time? How can I handle the problems, disappointments, and crushed expectations that surely will come?"

At one low point, I wrote these words:

Enough is Enough
What seemed like open doors
Have turned into repeated horrors.
I've tried, and tried, and tried,
Only to find my hands continually tied.
Constant aggravations
Slowed my imaginations.
Each renewed hope left my mind untethered,
Full of efforts to make future storms a bit more weathered.
But losses and changes signaled growing trouble,
Till they finally burst my faith-sustained bubble.
All my inner peace has now evaporated
And in its place is pain, exacerbated.
Silence, shame, anger, and mistrust
Have clawed my innards with merciless disgust.
I bleed from a thousand slashes.
'Till now my hopes are merely ashes.

Even an anvil with strong intents
Can be shattered by repeated dents.
Oh God, where have you been through all my disappointments?
Where are you now as I cringe under these deep bents?
Enough is enough
Of this never-ending stuff.
Why should I go on?
How can I go on?

Scores of times I spoke with God, even though most of the time it felt like a one-way conversation, as though I was talking to a brick wall. I murmured, "God, I'm afraid to ask again for your guidance, only to be burned again. I don't want to be shamed or left with the feeling that, somehow, my new efforts were in vain, as before."

Also, at this point I was reluctant to ask God for guidance on any new ideas. I worried that if I somehow initiated my own agenda I'd get disillusioned again, only to find my heart hardened toward him like the Jews of Old Testament times: *In the desert they gave in to their craving; in the wilderness they put God to the test. So he gave them what they asked for, but sent a wasting disease among them . . . Then they despised the pleasant land; they did not believe his promise. They grumbled in their tent and did not obey the Lord.*[8]

I wondered, "Why should I get my hopes up, preparing diligently for my writing plans or some other opportunity, when I'll surely face similar stumbling blocks?" I was skeptical toward God's future for me, and fearful to begin new projects or renew efforts on old tasks, lest I be let down again. My hope for the future had been dashed.

POINTS TO PONDER:

- Have you found that some Bible promises seemed worthless, like they were mocking you? Which ones?
- How has your thinking about God's character changed since you've experienced his abandoment or betrayal?
- In what ways has your outlook for the future changed?

SUGGESTED ACTION STEP:

Do a brief "spiritual autopsy." Write down some of the ways your relationship with God has been damaged by your faith crisis.

CHAPTER 4
EMOTIONAL DISTRESS LEADS TO
A NEW PERSPECTIVE

*All of life is an attitude. There are a lot of people who
feel sorry for themselves, and one thing I know for
sure is that pity parties will kill you. If you do have
one, dear, be sure to make it a short one.*

Dolly Parton

MY IMMEDIATE RESPONSE TO TERMINATING THE BOOK CONTRACT?
Profound disappointment, deep sadness, injured pride, explosive anger,
and escalating anxiety. As time went on, my inward hell stretched
way beyond its initial brief shock and continued relentlessly for more
than a year. My anguish over my losses resulted in two soul-damaging
emotions: resentment and depression.

RESENTMENT

The "Big Book" of Alcoholics Anonymous talks about the effects
resentment has on alcoholics, but it could just as easily be talking
about anyone simmering with anger. It teaches:

Resentment is the number one offender. It disturbs more alcoholics than anything else. From it stem all forms of spiritual disease . . . this business of resentment is infinitely grave. We found that it is fatal. For when harboring such feelings, we shut ourselves off from the sunlight of the Spirit. The insanity of alcohol returns, and we drink again. And with us, to drink is to die. If we were to live, we had to be free of anger. The grouch and the brainstorm were poison . . . The greatest enemies of us alcoholics are resentment, jealousy, envy, frustration, and fear. [1]

I was furious at God for misleading, tricking, and betraying me. I challenged him, "Do you get some kind of sadistic joy from operating with smoke and mirrors with your followers? Are you a mean, vindictive, sadistic being who delights in tormenting those whom try to trust and obey you? Do you even care about the confusion and heartache you've caused me?"

DEPRESSION

This resentment soon led to darker moods. I'd had a year's string of bad luck, and had become obsessed with frustrations, resentments, fears, self-condemnation, and self-pity. My previously "up" mood tilted helplessly down, and my dour outlook gathered speed like a car with no brakes, careening downhill on a winding mountain road.

Inwardly, I cried out to God to fix the setbacks and stop what I knew would escalate into depression. I was already experiencing many of its symptoms:

- Sleep problems: too much, too little, or fitful
- Extreme fatigue

- Lethargy: difficulty "moving off dead center"
- Procrastination
- Down on self, especially feeling self-blame and resentment
- Low self-confidence
- Poor concentration and memory
- Irritability, impatience, and temper explosions
- Obsessive thoughts
- Appetite changes
- Increased misperceptions, poor judgment
- Paranoia
- Isolating behavior and avoiding crowds and phone calls
- Negative attitude
- Lack of hope for future
- Risk-taking
- Suicidal thoughts

God's absence gnawed at me constantly. I ached inwardly, "I can't even pray. I'm depressed and agitated and tortured constantly—mentally, physically and spiritually. How can I free myself from this black cloud of sadness and boiling agitation that follows me everywhere?"

My mind uttered the words of the psalmist: *"My thoughts trouble me and I am distraught . . . I cried out to God for help; I called out to God to hear me. When I was in distress, I sought the Lord; at night I stretched out untiring hands, and my soul refused to be comforted . . . I was too troubled to speak."* [2]

MOVING FORWARD

Something had to change—this current misery was unbearable. I knew that moving beyond my negative circumstances would require me to reframe my losses, adjust my attitudes, and deal with my growing resentment.

Through the early months of 2008, I tried various methods to cope with my depression. I wrote about my frustrations, exercised, confided with close friends, talked with a therapist, studied my Bible, and read recovery literature.

To help me deal with resentment, I devoured books and articles, scoured the Internet for tips, interviewed others, prayed, and jotted down my thoughts.

My recovery was moderately successful, but I knew I still had to deal with the biggest problem: my damaged faith.

Philip Yancey has written several excellent books dealing with thorny issues, including faith crises similar to mine. One of his books, *Disappointment with God*, gave me some profound insights about the role of faith in dealing with dark nights of the soul.

Yancey reminded me that even Christ himself, God incarnate, went through an excruciating time on the cross, feeling entirely abandoned and forsaken by God. This meant Christ genuinely understood how I felt.

Yancey's book describes the choices available to people when trapped in a faith meltdown. I carefully considered my own version of each of them:

- I could ignore God by shutting him out of my life.
- I could spew my pent up anger against God for stringing me along and then deserting me.
- I could honestly express my pain and doubts to God and a few safe friends.

Looking over Yancey's options made me realize that, sooner or later, I had to act on one of four assumptions:

1. **I alone must make the best of my problems.** There is no personal, caring God. Life is pointless. I exist in a meaningless universe without any outside source of help.

2. **God simply can't be trusted.** Perhaps he has a mean, cruel streak that desires to punish those who cross him in some way. Maybe he deliberately provides deceptive guidance that shatters dreams. Maybe he gives out unclear advice to test people. Therefore, I need to depend solely on my own resources, because God simply cannot be depended on.

3. **I've been wrong from the start and I need to mend my ways.** Maybe I've misunderstood God's guidance. As closely as I've tried to follow his direction, maybe in my excitement I've twisted his words and have bent them to suit my own expectations. Perhaps there's something about my lifestyle that's offended him and has disqualified me from enjoying successes.

4. ***Both*** **God and I are right.** He's given clear guidance all along, and I understood and followed it correctly. But for some reason unknown to me, he's got a *better* plan. Maybe he's equipping me to offer relief to others who are gritting through similar seemingly divine abandonments and betrayals. Perhaps he wants to teach me lessons about relying on him, even when all outward circumstances appear to contradict his seemingly clear guidance. This means I'll need to trust that God has something better down the road for me, even though it clearly appears he's slammed several doors on me.

Rather than totally giving up on life and God, I decided to go with option four and "faith it" as best I could. I chose to believe that God was paving the road before me, using my losses as a teaching opportunity. I held tenaciously on to his promise: *"In all things God works for the good of those who love him, who have been called according to his purpose."* [3]

This decision caused me to reflect on the words of a small, painted card that I'd taped to the side of my printer:

Joseph
Of his plans—
All that was left
Was broken.
Yet, he learned
What was left
Was enough. [4]

Maybe, in my situation, God had to take some things away before he could replace them with something better. I remembered that Jesus described God as a wise gardener: *"He cuts off every branch in me that bears no fruit, while every branch that does bear fruit he prunes so that it will be even **more** fruitful."* [5] Reluctantly, I realized that God might be using my spiritual catastrophe to cut away excess baggage, preparing me for a greater journey ahead.

This new perspective was like a breath of fresh air for my book project, and I started working with vigor. Although I still encountered emotional potholes here and there, I believed God had finally given me solid, keep-working-at-it-Jim assurance. In the midst of frustrating computer glitches, email problems, and typist difficulties, God gave me the words to write a poem that encouraged me to persist:

My Task: Many Distractions versus One Focus

My task's been given, oh so clearly,

So why the stress that costs so dearly?

Obstacles abound;

Answers are not found.

I want to cry,

But I can't deny

That God above

Assigned this in love.

All I can do

Is trust his view.

The earth's scarred with hurting sheep,

Each one needing hope and sleep.

This book will rescue many,

If I don't let small crises slow it any.

God help me not to lose your ordered focus

By spending too much time on every locus.

Now I must keep to the task at hand,

So as to reach far more than just one small band.

THE POWER OF PERSPECTIVE

During this time of renewed focus, I came across another source of inspiration: a devotional from *Our Daily Bread*. It told a story about the impact of reframing a picture.

The anonymous author wrote about his experience of watching through a webcam a mama and papa eagle and their newly hatched eaglets in their nest. The parents took turns guarding and hunting for food for their offspring. One day, both parents disappeared, leaving their little babies alone in the nest.

The story's author watched intently through his webcam's lens, fearing that something horrible had happened to the parents. He worried, "How will the tiny, helpless chicks survive without food or protection from their parents?"

Then he reframed the picture by enlarging the camera's field of view to a wide angle . . . and there was Mama Eagle, perched close by on a tree branch, watching her babies' every move.

What an enormous difference it made to reframe the picture! The writer shared that he had often felt God had abandoned him, just like he had *wrongly* concluded the eagle parents had done to their little ones.

He could relate to the despair the small, frightened eagles might have felt when their parents left them alone in the nest, seemingly forever. But now he realized he needed to think of the *big* picture, the *whole* story, which he couldn't always see.

This story reminded me of a verse in Deuteronomy, in which Moses describes God as *"like an eagle that stirs up its nest and hovers over its young, that spreads its wings to catch them and carries them aloft."* [6] Just as eagles care for their young, so God cares for his people, even when they feel abandoned. Whenever I felt like I'd been abandoned or betrayed, I thought about the webcam story and reminded myself of the power of perspective.

POINTS TO PONDER:

- If you are going through a loss of faith, what are your current views about God?
- How might depression, resentment, or fear be clouding your view of God?

SUGGESTED ACTION STEP:

Try reframing your loss by writing a description of how you might begin to go forward despite your loss. What would things look like? Share your thoughts with a safe, reliable friend and ask for feedback.

CHAPTER 5
LESSONS I'VE LEARNED FROM MY FAITH CRISIS

Those things that hurt, instruct.

Ben Franklin

MARTIN LUTHER WROTE, "AFFLICTION IS THE BEST BOOK IN MY LIBRARY." Similarly, a Spanish proverb states, "Experience is not always the kindest of teachers, but it is surely the best."

Bad experiences can teach us valuable lessons, but only if we are open to learning from them. After months of inner turmoil, I finally reached a state of openness and learned a few basic, common sense truths:

1. Pain can be a great teacher.
2. Being cut off from God doesn't always mean you're at fault.
3. God often uses the worst times to produce the best results.

LESSON 1: PAIN CAN BE A GREAT TEACHER

Sometimes God calls us in one direction only to get us to a place where we can hear and respond to an even more important call. As a college student and new Christian, I felt called to go into medicine—until I faced chemistry. Even with the help of several tutors, all my frustrated efforts only earned poor grades. I was devastated—my whole vision for my life's career was unraveling. I thought my life was going to be in medicine, but God used the painful brokenness of my chemistry failure to open me up to a different career path: professional ministry. Had I gone into medicine, I wouldn't have been a good doctor. Nor would I have the ministry I do today.

And now, many years later, my writing obstacles have once again forced me to expand my trust in God's sovereign management. I'm learning to rely on him, even though I still don't understand why he directed me to follow a path that was strewn with wrecked dreams. Still, I believe he is good, whatever my current circumstances might be.

Because of this experience, when the next harsh blows come, I will be able to exercise a more patient confidence that, come what may, God will see me through. I will remind myself of Jesus's words describing the reality of life's problems: *"Things that cause people to stumble are bound to come."* [1]

What I used to see as destroyed dreams I now view as only temporary, surmountable obstructions, which are sometimes opportunities in disguise. I try to view a shut door or failure as a springboard to another project, a different calling.

Maybe God allowed me to flounder on my book project so that I could learn something from the obstacles—the see-sawing of faith and doubt certainly provided unsought wisdom. I now see that my unwelcome "seminar" in life's upsets was God's way of motivating me to work on a series of books.

Peter Marshall, former Chaplain of the U.S. Senate, felt the same way: "God doesn't permit any troubles to come upon us, unless he's got a specific plan to use that difficulty to also birth a great blessing."

Paul Abram Constantine shares his own helpful slant on disappointments, failures, and reversals: "I don't view them as defeats. I see them as *lessons.*"

I've been fortified to react to disappointments and other hurts by the words of the Apostle James: *"Consider it pure joy, my brothers and sisters, whenever you face trials of many kinds, because you know that the testing of your faith produces perseverance. Let perseverance finish its work so that you may be mature and complete, not lacking anything."* [2]

In some ways, my experience has mirrored T. S. Eliot's words in his poem "Little Gidding":

And the end of all our exploring
Will be to arrive where we started.
And know the place for the first time. [3]

Sometimes pain and crises are the only ways you and I can be equipped to move in a new direction—and find a new relationship with God. We can profit from our crises if we remain open to learning lessons from our pain. Are you willing to allow God to use your pain to refine you into the person he wants you to be?

LESSON 2: BEING CUT OFF FROM GOD DOESN'T ALWAYS MEAN YOU'RE AT FAULT

Can you relate to the words of the Roman playwright Platus, who said, "Nothing is more wretched than the mind of a man conscious of guilt"? I certainly can.

In my warped thinking, my book failure occurred because I

somehow let down God. I thought the failure was evidence that God was withdrawing his presence to punish me for my past sins.

In fact, the book of Jeremiah reveals that sometimes God's rejection and withdrawal *was* linked to the sins of his people:

> *While you were doing all these things, declares the Lord, I spoke to you again and again, but you did not listen; I called you . . . I will thrust you away from my presence . . . for [I have] rejected and abandoned this generation that is under [my] wrath.* [4]

Although a sinfully-stubborn heart sometimes plagued me, I didn't believe my thoughts and deeds were as bad as the rebellious actions of God's people in Jeremiah's time. They repeatedly and intentionally disobeyed his commands. And even if somehow my sins had been as evil as, or even worse than, those people, I relied on God's word: *"For I will forgive their wickedness, and will remember their sins no more."* [5]

But, for a long period, I believed the guilt-tripping accusations believers often use to shame others: "Your lack of awareness of God's abiding presence is alarming, frightening, even evil. You are cut off from God because you simply aren't living in harmony with him." These accusers claimed my sins had caused God to leave me. Yes, I agreed that I had sinned, like any other human, even repeatedly at times. But at each instance of disobedience, I'd confessed my transgression to God and sought his forgiveness.

As a redeemed follower of Christ, I knew my sins had been forgiven and that my sufferings were not the result of God's punishment. There had to be some other reason for God's seeming absence in my life.

As I reread the Scriptures and biographies of great men and women of faith, I discovered my experience wasn't unique. Nor was it tied to divine punishment for my poor decisions—God's withdrawal simply seemed to be a bitter reality of life for some people.

In fact, as the book of Deuteronomy records, the Israelites had to learn that their adversity was *not* a sign of God's abandonment for their transgressions. Moses reminded them that all along, despite their wretched, seemingly hopeless circumstances, God had been leading them throughout their forty years in the wilderness. And God promised to bless them if they kept his commandments during desert wanderings.

Living in a dark night of the soul does not necessarily mean you've sinned or failed in some way—countless godly people through the centuries have experienced the total lack of God's closeness.

LESSON 3: GOD OFTEN USES THE WORST TIMES TO PRODUCE THE BEST RESULTS

Several summers ago, I used a GPS for the first time when I was vacationing in Florida. It came with my rental car. My anxieties about my new electronic toy escalated as I drove out of the Orlando, Florida airport.

I knew I needed to head *west* to Vero Beach for a dinner meeting. Within minutes, the GPS told me to drive *east* toward Tampa.

I thought, "This can't be right, you stupid machine! Tampa's in the opposite direction of where I need to go. But my map's in the trunk. I can't stop in this traffic to grab it, so I have no choice but to rely on God to direct me." Then I prayed, "Lord, please use this GPS to get me to Vero Beach on time."

In spite of my urgent prayer, the GPS and road signs kept directing me to Tampa for the next twenty traffic-filled minutes. My foot may have been on the gas pedal, but my mind and hand were on the panic button.

I uttered a few choice non-Christian words and a quick version of the Serenity Prayer as I turned over my trip, the GPS, and my dinner engagement to God. Slowly, I transitioned from sheer panic to anxiety to peaceful resignation.

Soon my GPS angel told me to switch to a different highway. Suddenly, Vero Beach signs replaced signs to Tampa. I relaxed and obediently followed wherever the GPS indicated. And I arrived at the meeting on time.

This taught me a great lesson: at first, I thought the GPS was throwing me off track. Later I realized the GPS had the final designation in mind all along—and the seemingly wrong directions were a necessary part of its plan to get me on the right path. That incident reminded me that I have to have confidence that God sees the big picture for my life and will direct me to where I need to go. ·

I thought of the verse, *"Trust in the Lord with all your heart and lean not on your own understanding."* [6] Yet trust is not a once-and-for-all decision. I realize that each time in the future that I'm faced with adverse circumstances, I'll need to release the outcome to God's management.

A promise that's been of great encouragement to me is: *"I will lead the blind by ways they have not known, along unfamiliar paths I will guide them; I will turn the darkness into light before them and make the rough places smooth. These are the things I will do; I will not forsake them."* [7]

One faith-wrestler noted, "Trust in God seems to grow best in *poor weather*: very little sun or none, too much rain or too little, or inadequate fertilizer." And the singer and actress Dolly Parton once said, "The way I see it, if you want a rainbow, you gotta put up with the rain."

Letdowns, disappointments, and defeats are woven into the fabric of life, and to overcome these, sooner or later you have to depend on God's wise, loving control of your life's settings. Trust is an inner attitude that chooses to submit to the leadership of our caring, loving God, admitting that he knows best, even if at times his methods seem flawed.

POINTS TO PONDER:

- What key lessons have you learned from being cut off from God?
- Can you recall a bad event that turned out better in the end?
- While your present circumstances might seem to indicate God's displeasure with you, can you think of any evidence of his confidence in you?

SUGGESTED ACTION STEP:

Make a list of times when things were tough for you but ended up being a blessing.

CHAPTER 6
BENEFITS I'VE GAINED FROM MY RELIGIOUS MELTDOWN

Some defeats are more triumphant than victories.

Michael de Montaigne, Of Cannibals

SOMETIMES THERE ARE THINGS TO BE GAINED FROM SUFFERING. WRITERS in the Bible stated, *"Surely it was for my benefit that I suffered such anguish"* [1] and, *"He lifted me out of the slimy pit, out of the mud and mire; he set my feet on a rock and gave me a firm place to stand."* [2] Philosopher and writer Khalil Gibran observed that "out of suffering have emerged the strongest souls; the most massive characters are seared with scars."

All nice sentiments, but how, in practical terms, have I benefited from my scars? I've gained several things:

1. An increased gratitude toward God
2. A motivation to encourage others
3. The discovery of new spiritual exercises
4. A greater thirst for the Scriptures

English poet and Anglican priest George Herbert penned, "You have given so much to me, give one thing more—a grateful heart." These words often echoed my prayers to God.

The Greek playwright Aeschylus described his understanding of God's undeserved blessing. Aeschylus's words from *Agamemnon* describe my gratitude:

> Even in our sleep,
> The pain which cannot forget
> Falls drop by drop
> Upon the heart
> Until in our despair
> Against our will
> Comes wisdom
> Through the awful grace of God.

In his book *Thanks! How Practicing Gratitude Can Make You Happier*, Dr. Robert Emmons describes many of the benefits of showing gratitude. He shows that putting gratitude into action improves health, reduces stress, strengthens relationships, and makes us generally happier.

Dr. Martin Seligman, former president of the American Psychological Association, writes, "Life inflicts the same setbacks and tragedies on the optimist as on the pessimist, but the optimist weathers them better." [3] A new outlook of gratitude toward God reshaped my faith and left me better equipped to weather life's ups and downs.

Having an "attitude of gratitude" gives us a positive perspective on life. Cultivating this grateful attitude helps us to see our situation in ways that can reduce panic and open up our thinking to new solutions.

When we can see the positives as well as the negatives in our lives, it makes it harder to complain or remain stuck in resentment.

Being grateful also helps us realize the blessings we already have. It enables us to be content rather than always wanting things changed. It lessens our fear of always "missing out" on something better.

In her book *One Thousand Gifts: A Dare to Live Fully Right Where You Are*, Ann Voskamp notes that gratitude is a true anti-anxiety medicine. She writes, "It's impossible to give thanks and simultaneously feel fear." Think of this if you begin to feel anxious or start to despair.

Positive people find ways to stay grateful. Some people keep a gratitude journal. Some practice thanking God whenever they notice good things happening. Others develop a habit of every day giving at least one compliment to someone.

One way I developed a better outlook was thanking God every morning for three of his blessings of the previous day. This simple exercise has had an amazing effect on my mental attitude. I'm continually awed at God's unearned favor towards me, and for his amazing patience with my temper, doubts, cynicism, and waywardness.

BENEFIT 2: A MOTIVATION TO ENCOURAGE OTHERS WHO ARE STRUGGLING WITH THEIR FAITH

The Bible tells us that God *"comforts us in all our troubles, so that we can comfort those in any trouble with the comfort we ourselves have received from God."* [4]

D. T. Niles once defined evangelism as, "One beggar telling another beggar where to find bread." I like to remember this when I'm reaching out to support others facing faith crises. I listen patiently, share my story, and offer helpful resources.

Yes, it was horrible to endure those cheerless, secluded months of self-blame, resentment, fear, searching, and doubt. But now I have the strength and desire to reach out to Christian clergy and laypeople who are fighting their way through the same swamp of suspicion, anger, fear, skepticism, and distrust.

You too can use your experiences with doubt, failures, and successes to provide life-giving hope for other faith-strugglers. Even as your understanding of God continues to expand, and as you persistently work through your own faith issues, there will be plenty of God-sent opportunities to share your experiences. Don't feel like you need to wait until you've gotten every piece of the faith puzzle in place before you begin to share your faith battles and the lessons you've learned.

BENEFIT 3: THE DISCOVERY OF NEW SPIRITUAL EXERCISES

My faith crisis has changed my devotional life, leading me to do a few new things.

- Being a Type-A personality, I realized that I'm used to *doing* rather than *being*. To compensate for this, I'm experimenting with meditation exercises that clear my head and allow me to focus on maintaining a close connection with God.
- My devotional life will probably always be far less disciplined than my wife's and many others', but I've returned to more regular times of prayer and Bible reading.
- I find that listening to classical music frequently draws me into a special awareness of God's loving, power-filled existence.
- I take personal writing and renewal retreats several times a year to strengthen my relationship with God.
- To bolster my support system, I meet weekly in person or by phone with safe, encouraging friends for support, guidance, and camaraderie.

Your needs are obviously different than mine. Why not try out different forms of faith-nurturing to see what works best for you. Some of these methods might go beyond traditional prayer and Bible study. They might include: walking in nature, listening to music, playing an instrument, meditating, exercising, playing with pets, reading, painting, hanging out with friends, and many other methods. Use whatever brings you closer to God.

BENEFIT 4: A GREATER THIRST FOR THE SCRIPTURES

Bible reading and prayer are vital to a healthy spiritual life. If I skip reading the Bible for several days, I don't sense guilt, but I have a longing ache—like a water-starved man trudging across the desert.

My crisis has helped improve my regular habit of Scripture reading. I don't do it every day, but I find that I read more and more each week.

Discipline is required to achieve success in most areas of life: work, relationships, and hobbies. Why should it be any different with spirituality? A train might want to avoid the discipline of running on tracks, but without the rails' constraints, the train would quickly go off course or get stuck. After going off the rails during my spritual crisis, I've learned to make sure I stay on track, and Bible reading is the discipline that does it for me.

POINTS TO PONDER:

- Are you willing to explore some different ways of maintaining close contact with God?
- Do others see you as one who is quick to give God and others credit for the blessings you can still find in life, or do you grumble, complain, or blame?
- When you look back on your difficulty in two years, what will you be grateful for?

SUGGESTED ACTION STEP:

How about taking a risk? Try to initiate a conversation with someone who you sense is besieged by disappointments, filled with unresolved anger, overloaded with spiritual doubts, or worn down by unmet expectations.

PART TWO
GUIDELINES FOR SURVIVING A CRISIS OF FAITH

It is by those who have suffered that the world has been advanced.

Leo Tolstoy

INTRODUCTION

IF YOUR BOAT SINKS, YOU GRAB FOR WHATEVER WILL SAVE YOU FROM drowning: a life preserver, a life raft, or a plank of wood. Likewise, when your faith is collapsing, you'll need to use any strategy, any tool, that can keep your faith alive.

When my ruined dreams shocked my faith to the core, I used all kinds of survival recovery methods: I hummed words from hymns, recalled verses from the Scriptures, reread letters from family and friends, looked at family photos, went snowshoeing, rode my bike, walked my dog, watched upbeat movies, chuckled at newspaper cartoons, and visited my favorite practical joke store.

In my grueling hunt for answers, I learned much from the advice and examples of those who'd already trudged through similar desolate valleys. I hope you'll also benefit from the words and lives of faith survivors.

The following pages summarize what's been helpful for me and many others. I offer these options as recommendations—not as "shoulds" or "oughts," but as suggested guidelines.

As you experiment with these suggestions, I encourage you to apply a slogan like the one many 12-step groups use: "Take what works, and leave the rest."

GUIDELINE 1
REALIZE THAT MANY PAST HEROES ENDURED FAITH CRISES

Abide with me; fast falls the eventide;
The darkness deepens, Lord with me abide;
When other helpers fail, and comforts flee;
Help of the helpless, Lord, abide with me. [1]

Henry Francis Lyte

DO YOU FEEL THAT YOU OUGHT TO BE ABLE TO "FAITH IT" THROUGH YOUR disappointments like the others do? Or does it sometimes seem like no one else has experienced what you are going through?

It's helpful to remember that you are not alone in feeling abandoned and betrayed by God—countless other believers, past and present, have been through similar suffering. One of the keys to surviving and recovering will be remembering that you're not the only one whose faith has been stretched to the breaking point.

I found great relief through reading the accounts of faith-tested spiritual giants such as Thomas Aquinas, Oswald Chambers, William Cowper, and others who doggedly persevered through comparable mental suffering.

Years ago, the Spanish mystic and theologian St. John of the Cross wrote about his "dark night of the soul." Like St. John, countless saints throughout the centuries have ached with the psalmist who cried, *"Why, Lord, do you reject me and hide your face from me?"* [2]

In the late 1800s, poet, priest, and college professor Gerard Manly Hopkins regularly felt deserted by God. In his depressed anguish, he penned powerful poems of despair, one of which is called "Abyss" (also referred to as "No Worst, There is None"). I reflected time and again on a haunting line from that poem: "Comforter, where, where is your comforting?"

Perhaps the most famous faith-crisis sufferer was pastor and Protestant reformer Martin Luther, who often felt utterly abandoned by God and suffered unrelenting anguish and despair. During those dismal, lonely times, he persevered through periods of what he called *Anfechtung.*

While there is no English equivalent of the desolate word *Anfechtung*, Luther shared what these experiences felt like: "A trial sent by God to test man, or an assault by the Devil to destroy man. It is all the doubt, turmoil, pang, tremor, panic, despair, desolation, and desperation which invades the spirit of man."

Luther's battles with the dark nights of his soul frequently were accompanied by intense depressions. He felt that his depressions were somehow necessary. At the same time, they were dreadful and, by all means and in every way, to be avoided and overcome.

Roland Bainton, author of a classic book on Luther's life, *Here I Stand*, chronicled Luther's spiritual battle. Bainton quotes Luther, "The content of the depressions was always the same, the loss of faith that God is good and that he is good to me." [3]

After one of Luther's worst experiences of Anfechtung, he wrote,

"For more than a week I was close to the gates of death and hell. I trembled in all my members. Christ was wholly lost. I was shaken by depression and blasphemy of God . . . I dispute much with God with great impatience, and I hold him to his promises." [4]

Bainton describes Luther's core faith that sustained him in the midst of horrific inner turmoil, writing, "But always and above all else the one great objective aid for Luther was the Scriptures, because this is the written record of the revelation of God in Christ . . . He was completely lost unless he could find something without on which to lay hold. And this he found in the Scriptures." [5]

Amazingly, Luther suffered from God's absence most acutely *after* a special experience of God's grace: the highs of writing his *Ninety-Five Theses*. In 1527, a year of sickness and one of his worst depressions, he composed the great hymn of faith, *"A Mighty Fortress is Our God!"* Luther managed to keep his faith even during his great suffering. Luther processed his despair, and out of it have come hymns and writings that for centuries have continued to bless innumerable people.

As I read Luther's life experiences, I thought, "Wow. There's a ruthlessly-honest man who would understand my terrible plight." Knowing that my faith-testing wasn't a weird, isolated case relieved me of a lot of shame, guilt, and anxiety, and gave solid comfort in the midst of my loneliest times.

POINTS TO PONDER:

- Is it any reassurance to you to know that your faith crisis is not uncommon and that other Christ followers have plodded through their own versions of your misery?
- What can you learn from their struggles, defeats, and successes?

SUGGESTED ACTION STEP:

Read about a Christian hero who's suffered a faith crisis and see how he or she made it through.

GUIDELINE 2
KNOW THAT YOU'RE NOT ALONE—
FAITH CRISES ARE STILL COMMON

No temptation has seized you except what is common to man. And God is faithful; he will not let you be tempted beyond what you can bear.

1 Corinthians 10:17

IN ADDITION TO DISCOVERING THE FAITH-ENDURANCE EXPERIENCES OF saints from the past, I also found peace through knowing the stories of modern day faith warriors. Their experiences gave me invaluable hope, guidance, and inspiration at several critical times in my own faith battles.

THE WAR-WEARY CHAPLAIN

Captain Roger Benimhoff, a us Army chaplain, began his formal religious training at Southwest Baptist Theological Seminary in Fort Worth, Texas. He'd recently completed two tours in Iraq, and then accepted a position as a chaplain at Walter Reed Hospital working with wounded outpatients. Day after day, he counseled soldiers and saw much pain and death. As a result, his own faith was rocked to the core. He wrote in his diary:

The spiritual battle I am engaged in is a minute-by-minute war . . . Can [I] keep doing this? Is the pain and the heartache worth it? . . . I found myself getting violently mad at God . . . My God doesn't protect me and I feel vulnerable! . . . I do not want anything to do with God. I am sick of religion . . . I hate God. I hate all those who try to explain God when they really don't know.

Eventually he regained his faith:

This past year has been the most challenging of my life. But I have a new relationship with God. I tend to be more blunt with him . . . I'm dealing with anger toward God and grief over loss . . . God gave me room to cry out . . . He allowed me to slowly move through the mud and the mire . . . It's messy, it's not a pretty ending . . . I cannot tie a pretty bow on my story and I don't believe that God would want me to. [1]

THE IMPRISONED LEADER

Archbishop Desmond Tutu knew firsthand the tormenting loneliness of feeling like one of God's outcasts. His outspoken opposition to South Africa's unjust sufferings caused him to be imprisoned for years. He prayed and prayed for God to act to correct them. Seemingly, God didn't answer him.

In the midst of his seclusion, Tutu said, "We might have been forgiven for wondering whether God was around, whether God saw, whether God heard, whether God was even aware of the suffering and injustice and oppression. People detained, jailed, tortured. People exiled, people killed. All of this, it seemed, did not touch God." [2]

THE DISILLUSIONED ATHLETES

In the midst of a successful career as a major league baseball pitcher, Dave Dravecky had to have his throwing arm amputated due to cancer. All his years of preparation, his chosen career, his dreams—gone. He suffered through long bouts of depression and constant faith-testing. Finally, after finding professional help, caring acceptance from loyal friends, and much inner work, Dave triumphed over his pain. Today, as a result of his spiritual trial, Dravecky leads *Endurance*, a powerful ministry that aids cancer and amputee victims (and all kinds of other wounded people).

Another athlete, Dr. Henry Cloud, had passionately wanted to be a professional golfer since his late teens. He was convinced that's what God wanted him to do with his life. He practiced and practiced, but one day he injured his shoulder. The damage was permanent, and he couldn't resume golfing.

For some time, he was broken, disillusioned. Gradually, he discovered that God had something better in mind: counseling was to be his calling. How blessed we are that he never became a pro golfer—his counseling, writing, and speaking are terrific gifts to the Christian community and the world.

THE LIVING SAINT

Mother Teresa, Nobel Prize winner from Calcutta, was famous for her work among the the dying and the poor in India. Yet unknown to most, she suffered through spiritual agonies that lasted for decades.

A biographical book about her, *Mother Teresa: Come Be My Light*, consists mainly of almost seventy years of correspondence between Mother Teresa and her confessors and superiors. It covers her painful inner journey, which she describes as being dry, dark, lonely, and torturous. She compares her experiences to hell and says it drove her to doubt the existence of heaven and even of God. At the suggestion of a confessor, she wrote to Jesus:

> I have gone and still am going through hard spiritual trials . . . In my soul I feel just that terrible pain of loss—of God not wanting me—of God not being God—of God not really existing . . . Lord, my God, who am I that you should forsake me? The child of your love—and now become as the most hated one—the one you have thrown away as unwanted—unloved . . . I call, I cling, I want—and there is no one to answer—no one on whom I can cling, no, no one—alone . . . The darkness is so dark—and I am alone—unwanted, forsaken . . . In my heart there is no faith—no love—no trust—there is so much pain—the pain of longing, the pain of not being wanted. [3]

THE TRAGEDY-STRUCK PASTORS

A headline for a touching article in the *Los Angeles Times* read, "Facing Tragedy, Pastors Put Their Faith on Hold . . . Parent-Pastors Say God Let Them Down." [4] As pastors, Ronnie and Yvette Rodriguez had a ministry, Victory Outreach, which worked with recovering drug addicts and former gang members like themselves.

Yvette said, "I prayed and prayed for a little girl . . . When she came, I couldn't imagine how life could be any better."

From the start, tiny Alyssa brought joy and healing to her parents and to the men and women who lived with them in their church-run recovery home in Ontario, California.

On September 28, 2005, Ronnie and Yvette had to go to the nearby church office to install a computer. They left four-year-old Alyssa with a babysitter, Veronica Trejo, a forty-two-year-old churchgoer, mother of six, and a recovered methadone addict.

When they returned home, they found Alyssa—dead. "The coroner ruled that she had died of asphyxiation," wrote Claire Luna, a reporter for the paper. Trejo was charged with second-degree murder, accused of smothering Alyssa.

Soon after their child's death, Ronnie and Yvette started disengaging from their faith. They started by resigning as pastors.

At the time, Yvette said, "We had devoted our lives to helping people, then one of those people turned around and took away something so precious to us." She continued, "If this was some twisted test of my faith, I admit that I failed . . . God took everything from us. We have nothing left to give anyone else."

Her husband, Ronnie, mused, "Sometimes, I can't help but think God is punishing us for doing good . . . Then I think it's more cruel than that, that he wanted to get back at me for what I did when I was younger. He waited until I had Alyssa so that I would feel the most pain possible . . . You keep on wondering what could have been done differently . . . Maybe it was a mistake to devote our lives to this. Maybe we should have just let God do his work without us."

After a several-month trial, Trejo was acquitted. The loss of their daughter was bad enough, but this court ruling devastated the Rodriguez family and their friends. The trial's results brought deep frustration and a depressing sense of betrayal, leading the writer of the article to wonder, "How could they love a God who gave them Alyssa and then allowed her death?" The writer later noted, "And then came their doubt: maybe there isn't a God."

In spite of their terrible loss, Ronnie and Yvette slowly returned to worship, but they struggled with forgiving Trejo. Committing her into God's hands for judgment has given them some measure of closure to cling to: "Their conflict with the prosecutors over whether to pursue the other charges pushed them closer to God . . . Without any legal finality, they started to realize he might be their only source of closure . . . 'Veronica will be judged whether it's in this life or by God,' Yvette said, 'With nothing else to hold on to, we have to start believing that.' "

POINTS TO PONDER:

- Is it any support for you to know that your faith troubles are common to many of your contemporaries?
- What can you learn from their experiences?

SUGGESTED ACTION STEP:

This month, call or email someone who has survived a spiritual breakdown and ask what tactics he or she used to buoy up his sinking faith.

GUIDELINE 3
ALLOW YOURSELF TO GRIEVE

I feel how weak and fruitless must be any words of mine which should attempt to beguile you from the grief of a loss so overwhelming. But I cannot refrain from tendering to you the consolation that may be found.

Abraham Lincoln

GRIEF IS A UNIVERSAL, MULTIFACETED, AND PAINFUL PROCESS OF ADJUSTING to loss, whether it is a loved one's death, a major health issue, a job loss, or some other destroyed hope. Psychologist Maribeth Ekey describes grieving as, "Working through dead-end wishes that have not come true." [1]

Grieving is a perplexing and disorienting process that takes time to overcome. As one veteran griever says, "It is not something we get *over*, but rather it is something we get *through*." Elizabeth Jennings's poetic words described this painful reality:

Time does not heal,
It makes a half-stitched scar
That can be broken and again you feel
Grief as total as in its first hour. [2]

GRIEVING IS BIBLICAL

Most Christians readily accept the biblical correctness of positive emotions, such as joy, hope, and love. Yet none of us are immune to intense negative emotions like despair, anxiety, or bitterness.

In fact, many godly people in the Bible experienced a wide variety of harsh feelings: grief (2 Samuel 19:4), sorrow (Psalms 6:7), anguish and bitterness (1 Samuel 1:10), anger (Psalms 7:11), distress (1 Samuel 22:2), hopelessness (Psalms 42:5), fear (Matthew 14:26–30), and guilt (Matthew 27:3).

Jesus also grieved. When his close friend Lazarus died, the Bible records that *"Jesus wept."* [3] When reflecting upon his own upcoming death, Jesus lamented, *"My soul is overwhelmed with sorrow to the point of death."* [4] It is often comforting for grievers to know that, like them, Jesus had a reputation as *"a man of suffering, and familiar with pain,"* [5] who taught, *"Blessed are those who mourn, for they shall be comforted."* [6]

When we don't know how to handle our scary emotions, God has provided a roadmap with the book of Lamentations and the many psalms about grief. In fact, almost half the psalms are songs of grieving. And the writer of Ecclesiastes said, *"There is ... a time to mourn."* [7] Then, in Thessalonians, we are told that we *should* grieve, but not like those without hope. [8] When we simply can't express our confusion, numbness, frustration, upset, fear, rage, regret, and loneliness, God himself has given us the words from these honest biblical writings to use.

GRIEVING IS NECESSARY, EVEN CRITICAL

Too many Christians fail to adequately process their losses because they don't know the importance of grieving, or even how to grieve.

Some are shamed into speeding up their grief by well-meaning people who tell them, "Don't waste time being sad. God will use this for good." Others mistakenly believe that after a major catastrophe, God will take their sorrow away—if they are obedient to him and disciplined in their devotional lives.

Grieving people can get stuck in regrets, resentments, and aguish for years, never escaping their self-made prisons. Perhaps English Poet Richard Lovelace was referring to these internal incarcerations when he wrote, "Stone walls do not a prison make, nor iron bars a cage."

In my own processing, my daily, sometimes hourly, preoccupation with my unfair treatment jaded my thinking and relationships. In fact, nearly every area of my life was negatively impacted because I refused to stop nursing my wounds and mentally replaying hurtful emotions. I often found myself fueling my resentment, despair, fear, self-pity, or guilt. Sometimes I reacted in destructive ways, such as binge eating, withdrawing from family and friends, or making hurtful comments.

A closer look at these natural coping responses shows some of the ways they can be harmful to the recovery process if they remain unresolved:

- **Resentment** at yourself, others, or God can taint your outlook and relationships
- **Despair** that your conditions will not improve, or that your loss cannot be restored, can nose-dive you into a deep depression
- **Fear** that things will worsen can paralyze you from taking helpful actions
- **Self-pity** can become a vicious cycle leading to depression
- **Guilt** that you've made wrong or foolish decisions can torment you and ruin your bonds with others

Good grieving is necessary to restore emotional, spiritual, and physical health. Unless people adequately grieve their losses, they will stay prisoners to their past injuries, chained to their annihilated hopes, unable to fully embrace the present and future.

TYPES OF GRIEVING

There are plenty of books and articles on grief. One I've found helpful is *Unmasking Male Depression,* by Dr. Archibald Hart. [9] Although he gears his book toward men, women can also benefit greatly from his insights. Dr. Hart describes four types of losses:

- **Real, concrete losses** are things you can see, such as the loss of a loved one, a pet, or an expensive piece of jewelry.
- **Abstract losses** are creations of your own mind, including your self-esteem, someone else's love or respect, or plans for a future project. These are harder to resolve and usually require someone else to help you process your deprivation.
- **Imagined losses** are products of your imagination, sometimes with no basis in reality, such as a friend snubbing you, someone avoiding you, or people gossiping about you. But an imagined loss can be as wounding as a real one.
- **Threatened losses** may not have occurred yet, but they have the *potential* for scary, negative consequences. Examples include waiting for a medical biopsy report, a possible work layoff, a job performance review, or the outcome of an important legal proceeding.

It helped me to identify my visible and invisible losses. Only after I was able to pinpoint my "hurts" could I begin to explore more effective ways of coping and moving forward. Why not try to identify and categorize your unique losses? If you do, it can give you a head start in healing from your hurts.

Grief has many layers, and everyone processes pain differently. Most grief experts point to four stages of grieving, but people often don't go neatly and predictably through these major stages. Sometimes, people may struggle longer in one stage than another. At other periods, they may revisit a stage they've already gone through numerous times. Occasionally, they might skip a phase. But, although everyone is different, they will still experience each stage at some point.

The most common stages of grieving are:

1. **Denial:** a refusal to accept the loss. Maybe its reality is too hard to bear. This is why some people make repeated attempts to recover lost relationships, projects, or opportunities.
2. **Anger:** the feeling that you've been wrongly treated, which evokes resentment directed at yourself, others, or God.
3. **Depression:** the helplessness, hopelessness, and futility that set in as you start to think things won't improve. At times, you may blame yourself for your poor decisions. In addition to feelings of decreased self-worth, it's normal to experience depression as you grieve your lost plans. Although uncomfortable, this time of anguish helps you adjust to your broken dreams, and helps to reshape your perspective and your values.
4. **Acceptance:** the act of letting go, saying goodbye. Acceptance is an understanding, a tolerance, and an acceptance of the reality of

your destroyed dream. In this stage, you realize you can survive, even flourish, in spite of your tragedy.

Some people try to skip these stages to avoid dealing with their losses. They try to bury their hurt in a flurry of activities, by substituting another project, or by always keeping up a joyful "Christian front." But when sufferers avoid healthy grieving, their natural feelings of anger and despair escalate, paralyzing them.

I found that being aware of these stages gave me greater perspective on how I was coping with my wrecked hopes, and also helped me realize my reactions weren't crazy or unspiritual.

GRIEVE IN HEALTHY WAYS

There are, of course, scores of books on grieving. Likewise, many churches and communities offer grief support groups, but nearly all of these books and groups focus on coping with the death of a person or the loss of a marriage.

Unfortunately, few resources deal with grieving other kinds of losses, like a job terminated, a business venture soured, a partnership betrayed, or a college application rejected. Here are several suggestions from fellow grievers on how to mourn *any* kind of loss:

Allow Yourself Time to Deal with Wounded Feelings and Harmful Thinking

One thing is certain: grieving takes time. You can't rush it. The time needed generally depends on the severity of the loss—the greater the sorrow, the longer the grief.

There's no "normal" timetable for recovering from your losses. Go at your own pace. Sometimes your family, friends, therapist, pastor, or even your own Christian beliefs may try to shorten your grieving process by telling you to snap out of it. Don't allow their timeline, or even your own self-imposed pace, to rush your grief journey.

The Apostle Paul was well-acquainted with many zealous religious individuals. He knew that sometimes people's words and actions could cut deeply, even if they were well-meaning. He advised much caution when around such people: *"Let no one deceive you with empty words . . . do not be partners with them."* [10]

Reject their unhelpful statements. In their place, give yourself permission to be authentic about your feelings, whatever they are. Someone once told me I needed to allow myself adequate time to experience normal, human emotions, and not just ignore or fight against my feelings. This insight was very freeing for me—honesty about your feelings is one of the first steps toward recovery.

Write About Your Situation

Jot down a few phrases or sentences describing the disappointments, difficulties, and extinguished dreams you've endured. Describe your losses and include your feelings and thoughts, then share what you've written with an understanding person. This exercise has been a great blessing for me, and even played a large role in writing this book.

Use Whatever Method Gives You Comfort

Listen to music, soak in a hot bath, pet your dog, walk in the park, watch television, or look at old photos—do whatever soothes, or distracts you from doing negative replays. I personally enjoy riding my bike, painting, watching sports events on TV, and learning magic tricks. These comforting activities serve two purposes: First, they get our mind off our troubles. Second, they provide enjoyment, a critical component of recovery.

Surrender the Outcome of Your Broken Plans to God

When I got mired down in negatives, one thing that helped me was to pray and mentally apply the complete Serenity Prayer (attributed to Dr. Reinhold Niebuhr) to my specific circumstances:

> God, grant me serenity to accept the things I cannot change, courage to change the things I can and wisdom to know the difference; living one day at a time, enjoying one moment at a time; accepting hardship as a pathway to peace; taking, as Jesus did, this sinful world as it is, not as I would have it; trusting that you will make all things right if I surrender to your will, so that I may be reasonably happy in this life and supremely happy with you forever in the next. Amen.

This simple prayer exercise helped me see my disappointments in a new perspective. Try reading or praying the full Serenity Prayer whenever you begin to obsess over your injury.

Forgive Yourself and Others

One way to jump-start the healing process is to forgive the person or thing who ruined your hopes. If necessary, this also includes forgiving yourself. Dr. Lewis Smedes suggests three steps to forgiving:

1. See the offender as a flawed human being, a blemished person not much different from yourself.
2. Forfeit your precious right to get even, to punish, or to seek justice, and then choose to move on and treat the person with civility.
3. Ask God to give you the willingness to wish his blessing on the offender.

I followed Smedes's steps on an ongoing basis and found they relieved me of a lot of buried resentment and anxiety. What have you got to lose by trying them out for yourself?

POINTS TO PONDER:

- Have you allowed yourself adequate time to process your grief?
- How have you coped with small and large losses in your life? What helped? What didn't help?
- If you are going through a major disappointment right now, what stage of grief do you think you are experiencing?

SUGGESTED ACTION STEP:

Invest fifteen minutes a day trying a new way to handle your inner turmoil: writing or painting about your thoughts and feelings, taking a long walk, listening to comforting music, meeting with a friend to share your concerns, or any other coping method.

GUIDELINE 4
COME TO TERMS WITH YOUR LOSSES

Every branch that does bear fruit he prunes
so that it will be even more fruitful.

John 15:2

I KNEW I EVENTUALLY HAD TO COME TO TERMS WITH THE PAIN IN MY life, but I wasn't sure how to do it. I spent hours reading about how people successfully dealt with their big disappointments and I talked with others who'd made it through terrible situations. What I learned pointed me to one of the keys to my recovery: accepting the reality of my shattered expectations.

One of the primary teachings of Alcoholics Anonymous relates to acceptance. Consider this excerpt from the "Big Book" of Alcoholics Anonymous:

Acceptance is the answer to all my problems today. When I am disturbed, it is because I find some person, place, thing or situation—some fact of my life—unacceptable to me, and I can find no serenity until I accept that person, place, thing or situation as being exactly the way it is supposed to be at this moment. Nothing, absolutely nothing, happens in God's world by mistake.

The Big Book's passage on acceptance also apply to someone in a spiritual emergency, trying to recover from a significant loss:

> For me, serenity began when I learned to distinguish between those things that I could change and those I could not. When I admitted that there were people, places, things, and situations over which I was totally powerless, those things began to lose their power over me. I learned that everyone has the right to make their own mistakes, and learn from them, without my interference, judgment, or assistance!
>
> The key to my serenity is acceptance. But "acceptance" does not mean that I have to like it, condone it, or even ignore it . . . and I have to accept that fact.
>
> Nor does it mean that I have to accept "unacceptable behavior." Today I have choices. I no longer have to accept abuse in any form. I can choose to walk away, even if it means stepping out into the unknown. I no longer have to fear "change" or the unknown. I can merely accept it as part of the journey.
>
> I spent years trying to change things in my life over which I was powerless, but did not know it.
>
> I threatened, scolded, manipulated, coerced, pleaded, begged, pouted, bribed and generally tried everything I could to make the situation better—only to watch as things always got progressively worse.
>
> I spent so much time trying to change the things I could not

change, it never once occurred to me to simply accept them as they were.

Now when things in my life are not going the way I planned them, or downright bad things happen, I can remind myself that whatever is going on is not happening by accident. There's a reason for it and it is not always meant for me to know what that reason is.

That change in attitude has been the key to happiness for me. I know I am not the only who has found that serenity.

Nothing, absolutely nothing, happens in God's world by mistake. Until I could accept my alcoholism, I could not stay sober; unless I accept life completely on life's terms, I cannot be happy.

I need to concentrate not so much on what needs to be changed in the world as on what needs to be changed in me and in my attitudes. [1]

The AA's teaching on acceptance made sense, opening my eyes to a better way to approach my lost dreams. I knew didn't have to be happy about my losses, but I needed to become comfortable with their very real existence. Acceptance meant I had to come to the point where I was able to say, "This is reality, and even though I hate it, I can live with it," and, "My misfortunes were awful disappointments, and most likely, I'll not have another chance to redo them." Mentally, I had to accept the tough truth that I couldn't turn the clock back and have those same hopes again.

I needed to stop minimizing my damaged dreams, like when I'd tell myself, "These unexpected losses really aren't as bad as I make them out to be." And I had to stop rationalizing my grief by telling myself, "Others have it much worse than I, and I just need to buck up."

I also had to avoid unrealistic spirituality that included the wish: "If I just wait, hope, and pray, God will somehow resurrect my deflated dream." The only way I could move forward would be to let go of my goals, my plans, my concepts of what I'd believed God wanted me to do, and submit to his care, protection, and direction.

How do you move ahead without being bogged down by the hurts, failures, betrayals, bad choices, and regrets that are weighing you down? What's robbing you of joy right now? Is it a:

- recurring, upsetting thought about your loss;
- long-held dream that's been snuffed out;
- hard-worked-on plan ruined;
- severe, recurring health issue;
- soured relationship;
- failed business; or
- betrayal by person whom you trusted?

The only way to move forward is to let go of your past. Constantly reliving your upsetting situation anchors you to your pain. Each time you revisit old wounds, those memories can make you more afraid to move ahead, lest another hurt occur. You'll soon end up like a car stuck in the sand, its spinnning tires just digging deeper and deeper into a rut.

POINTS TO PONDER:

- Are you still clawing desperately, trying to "save" your loss?
- In what ways have you tried to minimize or unrealistically spiritualize your losses?
- Have you come to the place where you can really agree with the Serenity Prayer's phrase, "Taking, as Jesus did, this sinful world as it is, not as I would have it; trusting that you will make all things right if I surrender to your will"?

SUGGESTED ACTION STEP:

Each time you find yourself revisiting a past resentment, try calling a friend to share your responses, or write about your thoughts and feelings.

GUIDELINE 5
REACH OUT TO OTHERS FOR SUPPORT

No man is an island, entire of itself.

John Donne, Meditation VII

DON'T GRIEVE ALONE—IT HELPS TO HAVE SAFE PEOPLE WHOM YOU can share your burdens with. Sometimes it's helpful to talk with someone—a close friend, an understanding pastor, or a mental-health professional—who can empathize with your emotions and give you a balanced perspective.

The Bible encourages us to meet with others regularly for candid sharing and support. During my own spiritual worries, I remembered some of the Bible's many statements about the importance of caring for one another, such as:

Let us consider how we may spur one another on toward love and good deeds, not giving up meeting together as some are in the habit of doing, but encouraging one another. [1]

Two are better than one, because they have a good return for their labor: if either falls down, one can help the other up. But pity

anyone who falls and has no one to help them up! . . . Though one
may be overpowered, two can defend themselves. [2]

God has not designed us to live in prolonged remoteness. Rather, because we are made in his image, we are designed to be in meaningful relationships, living as a community. To ignore this reality, or to purposely shun this necessity during tough times, like during a faith crisis, can lead to increased spiritual, emotional, and psychological instability. In order to avoid this danger, I encourage you to reach out to others as much as you are able.

Tragically, perhaps the majority of American Christians live lonely lives, unconnected to other believers in close, reciprocally-caring ways. Their fellowship is merely a bumping of masks, never connecting on a real level.

It's a daunting task to find the right kind of supporters to share in your journey. Most people, including Christians, feel awkward around pain, whether physical, mental, or emotional. Some totally avoid you or change the subject each time you try to share your inner wounds. A few attempt to help. But their discomfort with physical, emotional, or spiritual suffering often leads them to offer useless, even toxic, words or actions, even though their motives might be right.

THE RISKS OF REACHING OUT FOR, AND CONNECTING WITH, SUPPORTIVE PEOPLE

We all need support from others. It's important to realize, however, that while fellow believers may try to be sincere and accepting, they may not be qualified to give spiritual-emotional advice.

The reality is that some of who you think will be helpful can actually harm you—those who've not already walked this path really cannot understand the deep, frightening issues you face. Because of this, it's helpful to keep in mind the risks that come from reaching out for empathetic people.

Vulnerability

In your pursuit of safe, helpful relationships, you need to be willing to be vulnerable. You won't find the reassuring people you are seeking unless you are willing to reveal your pain.

I struggled with this. I often had to talk myself out of being too protective of my reputation. I needed to become vulnerable and lean on nurturing friends. Sometimes I risked being judged when I mentioned that I'm really struggling.

Most people didn't know how to respond to my pain and immediately changed the conversation to a more comfortable subject. Some affirmed me with some kind of empathy, even if they didn't fully understand my situation or my feelings. Others offered shallow optimism: "Cheer up, Jim. Look at the bright side of things . . . every cloud has a silver lining . . . think of the glass as half full, not half empty."

Such clichés don't really acknowledge pain. They reach unrealistic, non-biblical conclusions that actually add to suffering. The Bible says, *"Like one who takes away a garment on a cold day, or like vinegar poured on a wound, is one who sings songs to a heavy heart."* [3] The words of these harmful helpers come across as platitudes or hurtful judgments, such as:

- Your loss isn't so bad; you shouldn't feel this way.
- Stop fretting, your situation is in God's hands. He's in control and all those matters will work out for good."
- You've got to be strong. God doesn't give us anything we can't handle.

- Take your troubles to God; he'll make them better.
- You need to find a way to get over this and get on with your life.

Seeking input from caring and non-judgmental people is both courageous and wise. Sometimes it takes grit and determination to seek safe relationships where you can open up. For me, it took immense courage to risk picking up the "10,000-pound telephone" to invite someone for coffee, especially knowing the potential for being hurt by a churchy person's overly-pious "spiritual stinger."

Avoidance

In the midst of suffering, many Bible heroes experienced considerable shame, blame, or avoidance from others.

The psalmist lamented, *"My friends and companions avoid me because of my wounds; my neighbors stay far away."* [4] and, *"I looked for sympathy, but there was none, for comforters, but I found none."* [5]

Agonizing over his multiple rejections, Job cried out his complaints about God's role in it:

> *He has alienated my brothers from me; my acquaintances are completely estranged from me. My relatives have gone away; my closest friends have forgotten me . . . they look on me as an alien . . . All my intimate friends detest me; those I love have turned against me.* [6]

Unfortunately, most people, including seasoned believers, can't handle the raw honesty of emotional pain. I expected support from most of my friends and fellow Christians. Yet they often avoided me when I attempted to share my faith slump because they were uncomfortable with my words, thoughts, and feelings.

Shame

Upon hearing my faith difficulties, some Christians accused me: "Jim, you obviously lack faith. In order to solve your faith problem, you'll need to read the Bible more, pray more, and simply claim God's promises for yourself. If that doesn't work, then you probably have some demons that need to be exorcised. You can come to our Thursday night exorcism service for that."

Others outright shamed me, saying, "Jim, you should be ashamed of your unspiritual reactions . . . Don't you believe Christ's honor-bound word that he would never leave or forsake you? You ought to have faith in him no matter what you feel. If your faith was genuine, you'd not have feelings of anger, bitterness, or doubt. Real Christians always have the joy of the Lord. Remember, Spirit-filled believers never question God. They accept the good and bad without complaining. Take heart and be joyful!"

Whenever I was around super-pious or judgmental church people, I winced inwardly and my stomach tightened. In these prickly situations, I identified with the words of poet Anne Sexton: "The world is full of enemies and there is no safe place." [7]

Blame

Some well-meaning friends reacted to my sharing with, "Jim, you must have done something really bad to deserve this kind of chastisement from God. What secret sin are you harboring?"

They were like Job's unhelpful friend, who said, *"Consider now: Who, being innocent, has ever perished? Where were the upright ever destroyed? As I have observed, those who plow evil and those who sow trouble reap it."* [8]

Oh, how those comments stung. But my introspection had led me to conclude that even though I was far from being the man of God I knew he wanted me to be, I hadn't sinned badly enough to deserve such terrible treatment from him. My response to my disconcerting "comforters" was, "Thanks for your thoughts. While I admit I'm a sinner like everyone else, I don't believe sin is the main reason for my soured plans and God's withdrawal."

But those stinging comments still reinforced my own inner thoughts: "Did I bring these things on myself? Perhaps Henri Nouwen was right when he said that the main obstacle to loving God is *service* for God. I may not have committed great sins, but perhaps my plans failed because I had been inadvertently forcing my own agenda instead of listening to God?

THE REWARDS OF REACHING OUT FOR, AND CONNECTING WITH, SUPPORTIVE PEOPLE

Carefully selecting others to walk alongside you can help in your healing. For example, a spiritual director, especially one who's personally gone through a similar dark season, can be a strong anchor during your storm.

Experiencing True Friendship, Fellowship, and Community

Friendship, fellowship, and community are essential to our spiritual journey. Nearly thirty-five years ago, I interviewed pastor-theologian Dr. Robert Munger about his best-selling booklet, *My Heart—Christ's Home*. I asked him:

Dr. Munger, many years have passed since you originally wrote your popular booklet. Since then, you've encountered many more life experiences and have received tons of worldwide feedback. Is there anything you'd like to change about your booklet?

I can still recall the gist of his reply:

> Yes, I certainly would! The single and most important revision I'd make would be to add another chapter called, "The Family Room"—a place where people can share openly and honestly. Christian fellowship, the simple act of knowing and being known, is a *necessity* for a well-lived life of faith.

Feeling Safe and Receiving Validation

It's *essential* for every Christ-follower, including clergy, to cultivate and use a caring support system of other believers. By sharing personal ups and downs on a regular basis, fellow believers can validate, comfort, guide, and exhort one another.

A line from *Macbeth* proves William Shakespeare understood the importance of verbalizing inner pain to trusted friends:

> Give sorrow words: the grief that does not speak, whispers to the over-burdened heart and bids it break. [9]

It's incredibly freeing to have someone safe to talk with, to share our messed up outlook on life, and to express the gut-wrenching fight that we're in. Friends allow us to shed our secret burdens. Being genuine with safe believers and non-believers is a liberating experience. I found that once I dropped my religious front that falsely communicated, "I've got my life and everything else under control," I was able to find true understanding and acceptance from many others.

Taking the risk and putting forth the effort to find empathetic people—who can encourage you in your struggles—will eventually pay off. Although it may take time and you'll suffer some letdowns, you will find in the midst of your trial a real gift: safe, supportive people.

Gaining Another Perspective through Wise Counsel

When my seemingly well-controlled world collapsed around me, it was easy to make wrong assumptions and rash decisions. I wanted desperately to throw anything at my problems that might fix them. How tempting it was to jump to conclusions, or to take actions I might later regret.

Rather than act on my own, I sought counsel from a few friends and from the writings of those whom I respected, including from the Scriptures. The Bible stresses the importance of seeking the advice of others when making substantial decisions:

Let the wise listen and add to their learning, and let the discerning get guidance. [10]

Plans are established by seeking advice; so if you wage war, obtain guidance. [11]

The way of fools seems right to them, but the wise listen to advice. [12]

Surely you need guidance to wage war, and victory is won through many advisors. [13]

Plans fail for lack of counsel, but with many advisors they succeed. [14]

Seeking an outsider's perspective is critical in a painful, numbing, and challenging time. If you've not yet shared your situation with others, take a chance and tell one or two people whom you consider trustworthy, wise, and practical. Their view from "outside the pit" can be very insightful.

POINTS TO PONDER:

- Have you reached out and shared your condition with anyone?
- Are you willing to become vulnerable by sharing your struggles?
- Do you have the courage to be misunderstood, shamed, or blamed if you're frank about your mental and spiritual condition?

SUGGESTED ACTION STEP:

Admit to yourself that you need a support system. Reach out and be open with your story. Take a risk by calling one or two non-toxic people to meet with and describe your inner war.

GUIDELINE 6
PRAY HOWEVER AND WHENEVER YOU CAN

Ah, Lord, my prayers are dead, my affections dead,
and my heart dead: but thou art a living God,
and I bear myself upon thee.

William Bridge

PRAYER CAN BE A REAL LIFESAVER IN THE MIDST OF SEEMINGLY UNENDING suffering, but you may not always feel able to pray. In those times, when God seems distant, and your prayers seem hollow and useless, remember this: pray as you can, however you can, whenever you can.

Hartley Coleridge expresses this well in his poem "Prayer":

Be not afraid to pray—
To pray is right.
Pray, if thou canst, with hope;
But ever pray,
Though hope be weak
Or sick with long delay;
Pray in the darkness,
If there be no light.

As you probably know, God invites us to communicate with him at all times. Even in our worst emotional-spiritual condition, he tells us, *"Call to me and I will answer you and tell you great and unsearchable things you do not know . . . always pray and [do] not give up."* [1] And the Bible tells us, *"Cast all your anxiety on him because he cares for you."* [2]

I was aware of the Apostle James's admonition: *"You do not have, because you do not ask God."* [3] But I was often so distraught over my circumstances that I simply couldn't motivate myself to pray and ask for help. Maybe you've experienced this difficulty as well.

Like many others, I'd prayed over and over for answers but never received any consoling guidance from God. Yet I knew prayer would be key in recovering my faith. I encourage you, despite all your hurts, to do the best you can to continue praying for healing, guidance, and courage to deal with your painful loss head-on.

ABANDON YOUR "NICE," THEOLOGICALLY-CORRECT PRAYERS

Scripture gives us permission to be brutally honest with God. For example, the psalmist voiced his soul-felt plea, *"I cry aloud to the Lord; I lift up my voice to the Lord for mercy,"* [5] and begged, *"Turn to me and have mercy on me; show your strength on behalf of your servant; save me, because I serve you . . . Give me a sign of your goodness."* [6]

Part of the spiritual maturation process of this rugged season of life is developing the ability to speak the hard truth to ourselves and to God. In this regard, Shakespeare's insight from *Coriolanus, Act III* is practical and helpful: "What his breast forges, that his tongue must vent."

It is psychologically and spiritually sound to vent your feelings with God. Tell him about your angry, skeptical, disillusioned, despairing, injured feelings toward him, others, yourself, and life. Yell, scream, cry, shake your fist, or stomp your feet.

In the midst of my uncertainty, I prayed:

God, open my eyes to your perspective on my disappointments. Help me hang on to your promises even though it seems you've locked the doors on the hopes, dreams, and plans I believed were from you. Help me to not let these lost goals blight my life with self-pity, resentment, and cynicism. Don't let me give in to despair. Protect me from giving up. Give me insights on how to rise above my mental suffering. Strengthen me with a hope that comes from viewing life from your eternal perspective. Teach me lessons that will help me stay the course. I want my whole life to be one long, obedient response of love for you. Please give me courage to do what you tell me.

Several years later, I penned this two-way prayer conversation with God:

Jim to God—

Oh, God of pain and shattered plans, I've tried to do what I believed was an assignment from you. But all I've gotten have been doors slammed in my face, and one disappointment after another.

I've prayed and prayed for help, for explanations, for guidance. But no answer from you. Only the silence of your seeming abandonment and betrayal. Something's not right with how you guide people.

I'm angry and tense and afraid and painfully alone. Seems like I'm totally by myself in an empty, meaningless universe, silently dangling from a rope, whipped about on an ink-black night by constant wind gusts.

I'd give anything to escape this terrifying feeling. Already, I've endured multiple tests of my once-strong but now-fragile faith.

God, I've not sensed your presence in any of these faith-traumas. Are you really here with me, right now? Even now, as I pray, I don't feel you near me. Where's the clear guidance, the peace you promised, especially in times like these? You've got to make your instructions clearer, your presence more obvious.

Can this lonely, ice-cold, black muteness be your domain as much as a joyful, Spirit-filled church is? Are you controlling events for my well-being—or ruining my life? Do you really care?

Or do you show up only at beach sunsets, or when healthy babies are born, or during soft, fresh snowfalls, or with stunning rainbows, or on cold winter nights around toasty family fireplaces, or through the compliments of friends, or while two lovers gaze into each other's eyes, or as church choirs sing inside tall steeple buildings?

I need to know if you can still bring some good from my hard work, high hopes, and crumbled plans, God. Because all my best efforts have failed miserably.

Now I have no one else to turn to. My family's nearby, yet they might as well be a galaxy away. Most of my friends and others don't understand my situation . . . or won't take time to listen. Many avoid me. Others offer hasty spiritual clichés, or they pile stinging shame on me.

So, it's just you and me against life itself in an unfair, unpredictable, uncaring world of both believers and non-believers. Can't you see I'm helpless to deal with my crushed expectations and non-supportive humans?

I'm facing deadlines and immense financial pressures. I need you, God. Please help me through this ordeal. Somehow, salvage my dreams and my plans, and restore my trust in you.

I pray this in Jesus's name. Amen.

God to Jim—

Yes, Jim, I've heard your prayer. I'm deeply touched by your frustrations, anger, and uncertainties. Please try to remember that even though you may not feel close to me, I'm always with you—in your hopes and in your disappointments, in your successful plans and in your unsuccessful attempts, in your doubts and in your faiths, in your angers and in your joys, in your obedience and in your sin. I love you! I proved it when I sent my son to be executed in your place for all your sins—past, present, and future.

Let me remind you, my special son, of what my book says about your birth and death: *"You created my inmost being; you knit me together in my mother's womb . . . your eyes saw my unformed body; all the days ordained for me were written in your book before one of them came to be."* [7]

Here are a few other things I've told you concerning our relationship :

The Lord will guide you always; he will satisfy your needs in a sun-scorched land and will strengthen your frame. You will be like a well-watered garden, like a spring whose waters never fail. [8]

Do not fear, for I have redeemed you; I have summoned you by name; you are mine. When you pass through the waters, I will be with you; and when you pass through the rivers, they will not sweep over you. When you walk through the fire, you will not be burned. [9]

Never will I leave you; never will I forsake you. [10]

Forget the former things; do not dwell on the past. See, I am doing a new thing! Now it springs up; do you not perceive it? I am making a way in the wilderness and streams in the wasteland. [11]

Neither death nor life, neither angels nor demons, neither the present nor the future, nor any powers, neither height nor depth, nor anything else in all creation [job termination, failed projects, cancer, heart disease, diabetes, mental illness, surgeries, or your sins] can separate us from the love of God that is in Jesus Christ, our Lord. [12]

Do not be afraid, for I am with you. [13]

I am with you always [Even when you don't feel my presence]. [14]

He will not let your foot slip—he who watches over you will not slumber; indeed, he who watches over Israel will neither slumber or sleep . . . The Lord will keep you from harm—he will watch over your life; the Lord will watch over your coming and going both now and forevermore. [15]

Jim, this terrible upset will pass. There will still be potholes in the road as you travel through life. But in spite of them, I will still be watching over you, my beloved son. Now, as you pick up the pieces of your shattered expectations, rebuild, and go on with your life, I will always be with you. My Holy Spirit will be your constant, invisible companion. One day, you will come to the end of your days and experience earthly "death." Even then, I will still be alongside you, comforting, guiding, encouraging you through my presence, my written promises, and my people.

Then, as you enter your new life eternal, I'll be waiting to welcome you into your real home, which I long ago prepared for you. You'll experience a dream-come-true reunion with your Christian loved ones. You'll receive your "Well done" and other wonder-filled rewards for your faithfulness in my work.

So Cheer up! Go on with your life. Keep using your skills and experiences to be my voice, my hands and my feet . . . until I call you to your permanent, eternal home in heaven.

With all my love and grace,

Your Perfect Heavenly Father

PRAYING IN THE MIDST OF YOUR FAITH RUPTURE

Sometimes, when I couldn't find the words to pray, I found it helpful to use the prayers of other Christians. Thankfully, faith-battlers who have gone before us recorded many of their prayers in the Bible, hymnals, and other writings. Have you ever considered adopting some for your own needs? For example, the Lord's Prayer is simple yet profound, and is one that countless Christians use as a jumping off point.

But sometimes I hurt so much that I couldn't pray at all. After long periods of prayerlessness due to my inner chaos, I realized that until I was in a better emotional place to pray, I needed to ask friends to pray for me.

I enlisted a few safe individuals to pray for me on a regular basis, explaining my faith issue and that I was currently "out of commission" spiritually. I let them know my concrete and immediate prayer needs, and I kept them posted as things developed—the good and the bad.

It's also important to remind yourself that right now the Holy Spirit is praying on your behalf. Scripture encourages, *"In the same way, the Spirit helps us in our weakness. We do not know what we ought to pray for, but the Spirit himself intercedes for us through wordless groans. And he who searches our hearts knows the mind of the Spirit, because the Spirit intercedes for God's people in accordance with the will of God.*" [16]

Jesus is also interceding for you. In times when you can't pray for yourself, remember God's familiar reassurance: "*Christ Jesus who died—more than that, who was raised to life—is at the right hand of God and is also interceding for us. Who shall separate us from the love of Christ? Shall trouble or hardship or persecution or famine or nakedness or danger or sword?*" [17]

POINTS TO PONDER:

- Do you know someone who couldn't pray because of his or her circumstances, but finally was able break through and talk with the God of Silence?
- Have you given up on praying about your condition?
- Can you be utterly honest with your anger and fear as you whisper, talk, yell, or scream out to God?

SUGGESTED ACTION STEP:

Even though God is silent and seems absent, uncaring, and unreachable, try spending five minutes a day reaching out to him. Use spoken, yelled, sung, thought, or written words to explain to him exactly how you feel.

GUIDELINE 7
THINK RATIONALLY AND LOGICALLY, NOT JUST SPIRITUALLY

I balanced all, brought all to mind.

William Butler Yeats

HAVE YOU EVER NOTICED THAT SOME CHURCH PEOPLE ARE SUPER-SPIRITUAL—nearly every sentence they utter has "God" in it? The witty remark about these folks is sad but true: "They're so heavenly-minded they're no earthly good."

Perhaps you've been looking at your problem only from a spiritual perspective. While this can be helpful, it can also be limiting and lead to religious tunnel vision. Sometimes, in addition to viewing things from a biblical perspective, thinking objectively and using common sense are what people need to get their faith back on track. The Bible teaches the value of reason, saying, *"Stop thinking like children . . . in your thinking be adults."* [1]

JUST AS THOSE IN THE BIBLE, ACTIVELY LOOK FOR ANSWERS

Jesus taught, *"Ask and it will be given to you; seek and you shall find; knock and the door will be opened to you."* [2]

The Bible tells us to think critically about our situation, reminding us that *"a prudent man gives thought to his steps,"* [3] and teaches, *"Love the Lord your God with all your heart and with all your soul and with all your **mind**."* [4]

Some of the Bible's greatest characters repeatedly sought answers for their problems. When physically, emotionally, and spiritually savaged by his undeserved suffering, Old Testament hero Job desperately sought the reasons for his misfortunes. More than forty times he cried out, *"Why, God?"* Yet God never explained why Job had to go through such awful tragedies. The Apostle Paul prayed three times for the "thorn" to be removed from his flesh, but God never granted these pleadings, only responding that his grace would be sufficient for Paul to overcome his suffering. In these and other cases, God didn't answer prayers or give his reasons for the sufferings of his people.

Although God challenges you and me to seek after the truth, he also gently reminds us, *"For my thoughts are not your thoughts, neither are my ways your ways . . . As the heavens are higher than the earth, so are my ways higher than your ways and my thoughts than your thoughts."* [5]

Even the disciples didn't always understand God's methods. For example, before washing his disciples' feet, Jesus had to explain to them, *"You do not realize now what I am doing, but **later** you will understand."* [6]

As I tried to find answers for my pains, I had to conclude that I'd probably have to wait until I get to heaven for God's explanations. But while God may not always explain the purpose of what has happened, he will never scold you for seeking the truth. Even the risen Jesus invited Thomas, his doubtful disciple, to verify his crucifixion wounds.

ANALYZE YOUR FAITH FOR FALSE ASSUMPTIONS AND BELIEFS

God often uses turbulent times to reveal false notions rooted in our belief system. In some ways, this was true for me. In my efforts to make sense of painful life events, I began to take a hard look at my long-held convictions. I noticed that many of my disappointments were based on unrealistic expectations of how God works.

Here are some common beliefs that periodically tainted my thinking—and could be coloring yours as well:

- Life is supposed to be good and fair—at least most of the time.
- God is in control, and he won't let serious tragedy happen to me.
- I'm trying hard to be a good Christian, so he won't let me suffer too much.
- My family and friends will support me if I'm suffering.
- I'll always feel God's presence, even when I'm hurting in some way.
- If I have enough faith, God will answer my prayers for healing, for guidance, and for help.
- If God doesn't solve my problem and make things right, it's because I don't have enough faith or my sins have short-circuited his desire to intervene on my behalf.

These and other assumptions were developed before my faith free-for-all. But during my crisis, as I reviewed these flawed ideas and their influence on my outlook, it became clear how wrong they were, and how much they hurt me. By discovering my unbiblical beliefs, I was able to develop a maturer, more realistic faith.

When life experiences contradict your expectations, it may be time to re-examine your faith to see if inaccurate beliefs may be contributing to your lack of understanding.

POINTS TO PONDER:

- What false religious ideas have you bought into?
- How are these pseudo truths influencing your thoughts, emotions, and actions?

SUGGESTED ACTION STEP:

Take a half hour to evaluate your current beliefs about God. Do this by reading, researching, and discussing your thoughts with a few safe people.

GUIDELINE 8
SEEK NEW PERSPECTIVE FROM THE BIBLE AND OTHER SOURCES

It was good for me to be afflicted
so that I might learn your decrees.

Psalms 119:71

BY SEEKING OTHER PERSPECTIVES, YOU'LL BE ABLE TO BETTER UNDER-stand your own adverse circumstances. In the midst of my long ordeal, the Bible, of course, topped my list of resources. Often, I searched it and found a new dimension of God's love and commitment to me. During those special periods, my Bible provided a welcome input of comfort, guidance, and courage. At other times, I found strength from different places. I watched films, read poetry, and listened to music. Many of these sources told stories I could relate to, and I found peace in knowing other people had gone through similar experiences to mine.

SEEK THE BIBLE'S PERSPECTIVE ON YOUR LOSS

I often found verses in Scripture that kept me going. One paraphrase of a New Testament verse stuck with me and infused me with courage to keep trudging through the mist: *"The hope that you have in our*

Lord Jesus Christ means **sheer dogged endurance** in the life that you live before God." [1]

I learned to use biblical statements as positive anchors in my storm-filled moments. These words proved to be a solid asset, loaded with upbeat thinking for my invisible war:

Dear friends, do not be surprised at the fiery ordeal that has come on you to test you, as though something strange were happening to you. But rejoice inasmuch as you participate in the sufferings of Christ, so that you may be overjoyed when his glory is revealed. [2]

Be made new in the attitude of your minds. [3]

The cheerful heart has a continual feast. [4]

Whatever is true, whatever is noble, whatever is right, whatever is pure, whatever is lovely, whatever is admirable—if anything is excellent or praiseworthy—think about such things. [5]

Scripture became a beacon for me. At times, familiar passages took on brand-new meaning and injected me with renewed inspiration:

The Lord upholds all who fall and lifts up all who are bowed down. [6]

I consider everything a loss because of the surpassing worth of knowing Christ Jesus my Lord, for whose sake I have lost all things. I consider them garbage, that I may gain Christ. [7]

Blessed is the man who perseveres under trial, because having stood the test, that person will receive the crown of life that the Lord has promised to those who love him. [8]

Like a drowning man clings to a life-preserver, I often hung to promises like:

Can a mother forget the baby at her breast and have no compassion on the child she has borne? Though she may forget, I will not forget you! See, I have engraved you on the palms of my hands; your walls are ever before me. [9]

The Lord is close to the brokenhearted and saves those who are crushed in spirit. [10]

For I know the plans I have for you . . . Plans to prosper you and not harm you, plans to give you hope and a future. [11]

However, most of the Scriptures don't offer explanations of current suffering, nor do they provide a detailed blueprint of God's plan. But they do reveal the caring, loving character of a kind and good God.

I could relate to pastor Warren Wiersbe when he explained, "Nothing is harder to heal than a broken heart, a heart shattered by experiences that seem so meaningless. But God's people don't live on explanations; God's people live on his promises." [12] When it seems like we've got nothing left, we still have hope in God's promises.

Still, in spite of the Bible's marvelous promises, there may be times when they simply won't be enough to steady your unbalanced thinking. At times this was true for me. Yet, over all, the Scriptures helped me to reframe my losses and to strengthen my will to endure.

Key statements from the Bible can provide a helpful long-term perspective as you begin to reframe your setbacks. This certainly was true for me as I remembered that God offered a future reward if I hung in there during my duress:

Though now for a little while you may have had to suffer grief in all kinds of trials. These have come so that your faith—of greater worth than gold . . . may result in praise, glory and honor when Jesus Christ is revealed." [13]

Like the Old Testament hero Jacob, I gradually came to realize that *"surely the Lord is in this place, and I was not aware of it."* [14]

IN ADDITION TO THE BIBLE, EXPLORE OTHER SOURCES FOR GUIDANCE

Like the advice to "diversify" your investments, you may find that certain books and web resources complement your Bible's teachings.

I found encouragement and direction from all sorts of secular and religious books, magazines, poems, songs, classical music, and movies.

Throughout my prolonged misery, I read or reread relevant books, such as Victor Frankl's *Man's Search for Meaning*, Phillip Yancey's *Disappointment with God*, Lewis Smede's *Keeping Hope Alive*, and John Mason's *Don't Wait for Your Ship to Come In: Swim Out to Meet It!* These and other books sparked a desire to *do* something about my situation rather than continuing to boil inwardly or freeze in fear.

I also gleaned some valuable lessons from seasoned leaders, writers, and thinkers:

- *Abraham Lincoln, US president:* "The best way to predict your future is to create it."

- *James Thurber, author and humorist:* "Let's not look back in anger, nor forward in fear, but around in awareness."
- *Soren Kierkegaard, Danish philosopher and theologian:* "To dare is to lose one's footing momentarily. To not dare is to lose oneself."
- *Mohandas Gandhi, Indian civil rights activist and leader:* "You may never know what results come from your actions. But if you take no action, there will be no results."

Above all, in spite of my disintegrated plans, I wanted to avoid being like the person in this piercing poem by an unknown author:

> Spring is past,
> Summer is gone.
> And my song that I was meant to sing
> Is still unsung.
> I have spent my days
> Stringing and unstringing my instrument.

Nor did I want to bear the reality of John Greenleaf Whittier's heartbreaking words:

> For of all the sad works of tongue and pen,
> The saddest of these: "It might have been."

These and other resources helped give me new guidance about my situation. They made me realize that I could overcome my faith trauma, and that I didn't want my life to be frittered away or to see my skills and efforts wasted. They helped me to look at other ways of making my life count—by helping, encouraging, and guiding others.

POINTS TO PONDER:

- In what ways has the Bible comforted you? How has it shaped or stretched your perspective on the painful circumstances you're going through?
- Besides the Bible, what other resources, such as literature, websites, videos, or classes have you explored?

SUGGESTED ACTION STEP:

Write down on a card a Bible passage that offers you encouragement. Read it out loud every day.

GUIDELINE 9
EXPAND YOUR UNDERSTANDING OF GOD AND HOW HE WORKS

When it is dark enough, men see the stars.

Ralph Waldo Emerson

A PRAYER OF SUSANNA WESLEY, MOTHER OF 18TH CENTURY CHURCH reformers John and Charles Wesley and seventeen other children, touched me deeply: "Help me, O Lord, to make a true sense of all disappointments and calamities in this life, in such a way that they may unite my heart more closely with you."

For reasons known only to God, some Christians must traverse relentless conflicts in order to keep their faith growing. Oh, how grateful I am that God finally allowed me to see my life and him in a new light.

While it seems simplistic, I've come to accept the old cliché: "God is in the refining business." Our journey through life will give us situations that will challenge our dearest, most tightly held human perspectives.

An anonymous writer observed, "Each time our world is shaken up, we'll be confronted by the need to reevaluate some point of our perspective on life and God. The murkiness from this chaos can sometimes 'fertilize' faith and nurture increased intimacy with God."

A lot of the spiritual devastation I experienced was connected to my incorrect ideas of what I thought a relationship with God would be like. My notion was that, for the most part, I would have a continual sense of his invisible hand on my shoulder. I believed that even in the toughest times, the awareness of God's presence would bring me calm, serenity, and real joy.

But this was definitely not the case during my darkest hours. Rather than having some kind of consolation, some sort of explanation for my hurts, God kept completely silent. I had absolutely no sense of his presence. In the place of peace, I experienced only anger, apprehension, and chaos.

In a committed relationship, you have someone with whom you can do battle. During our nearly five decades of marriage, when my wife, Leah, says or does something that hurts or angers me, I bring it up, and we discuss it—or argue about it. Although we've had our times of strife with each other, she's always there. Sometimes I even understand her! But what I discovered is that God doesn't always operate according to a human relationship model. He can be an elusive "partner" who doesn't speak up, talk back, offer explanations, or provide comfort.

RE-EXAMINING YOUR NOTIONS OF GOD IS NORMAL AND A SIGN OF A MATURING FAITH

Many Christian heroes have had their faith shaken up, reevaluated, and eventually renewed by an enlarged understanding of God and how he works. Questioning is part of the process of gaining a deeper understanding of God and his ways. Albert Einstein once said, "The important thing is not to stop questioning." This certainly holds true for followers of Christ.

For example, pastor, lawyer, and poet John Donne suffered one terrible calamity after another. In the midst of his suffering, he had to admit he didn't understand what God was doing, and he began to examine all that he'd previously understood about God. In *Devotions*, he wrote:

> I can read my affliction as a correction, or as a mercy, and I confess I know not how to read it. How should I understand this illness? I cannot conclude, though death conclude me. If it is a correction indeed, let me translate it and read it as a mercy: for though it may appear to be a correction, I can have no greater proof of your mercy than to die in thee and by that death to be united with him who died for me.

Part of the Catechism of the Catholic Church teaches:

> Illness can lead to anguish, self-absorption, sometimes even despair and revolt against God. It can also make a person more mature, helping him discern in his life what is not essential so that he can turn toward that which is. Very often illness provokes a search for God and a return to him. [1]

In a series of excerpts from his "Baffled to Fight Better" lecture, Oswald Chambers, Scottish Baptist, evangelist, and teacher, wrote:

> There are things in our heavenly Father's dealings with us which have no immediate explanation. There are inexplicable providences which test us to the limit.

Reason is our guide among the facts of life, but it does not give the explanation of them. Facing facts as they are produces despair, not frenzy, but real downright despair, and God never blames a man for despair. The basis of things is not reasonable, but wild and tragic, and to face things as they are brings man to the ordeal of despair.

Despair is the hopelessness that over takes a sane mind when it is pushed to the extreme in grief. When a man gets to despair he knows that all his thinking will never get him out, he will only get out by the sheer creative effort of God, consequently he is in the right attitude to receive from God that which he cannot gain for himself.

Trouble always arises when men will not revise their views of God.

To be an agnostic means I recognize that there is more than I know, and that if I am ever to know more, it must be by revelation. A Christian is an avowed agnostic intellectually; his attitude is, "I have reached the limit of my knowledge, and I humbly accept the revelation of God given by Jesus Christ."

Never be afraid if your circumstances dispute what you have been taught about God; be willing to examine what you have been taught.

Faith in God is a terrific venture in the dark; I have to believe that God is good in spite of all that contradicts it in my experience. It is not easy to say that God is love when everything that happens actually gives the lie to it. Everyone's soul represents some kind of battlefield. The point for each one is whether we will hang in, as Job did, and say, "Though things look black, I will trust in God."

from The Complete Works of Oswald Chambers

YOUR UNDERSTANDING OF GOD WILL CHANGE OVER TIME

The understanding of God that I had as a child, as a new Christian in college, as an adult, and now as an older man, has changed over time. Ten years from now, I'm sure some of my views will be different as well.

Although I didn't realize it, my early thinking as a youth and young adult had been limited by my preconceptions about God and how he worked: If God was silent, he must be uncaring, or punishing, or absent. And if my understanding of his will was thwarted, it meant he didn't care or he was somehow punishing me. I needed to let God's statement sink in: *"See, I have refined you, though not as silver; I have tested you in the furnace of affliction . . . I am the Lord your God, who teaches you what is best for you, who directs you in the way you should go."* [2]

The predictable, manageable box that I'd kept God in for most of my life has been ripped apart. I've been forced to adjust my "theologically-correct," comfortable, and safe ideas about God and how he works. Looking back, I believe my adversities have led to a more balanced view of God, his character, and his ways.

YOUR FEELINGS OF GOD'S ABSENCE MAY LINGER

Another scary reality is that maybe God is okay with you believing that he has absented himself from your life. King Solomon once noted, *"The Lord has said that he would dwell in a dark cloud."* [3] And

God refers to himself as being both close and far away: *"Am I only a God nearby . . . and not a God far away? . . . Do I not fill the heaven and earth?"* [4]

Some people are stuck in the faith fog for a long time, possibly for months or even years. In these dreary time, the only way to cope is to somehow copy a child's faith: a simple inner acceptance that God is there and that he cares.

I knew the fallout from my recent losses might continue for a long time. And I also knew God might not intervene to help me deal with my responses to them. I had to choose whether I was going to panic, boil with resentment, or freeze with fear, or if I was going to count on the fact that some way, somehow, God was in the strange mix of my chaotic circumstances. Eventually, I chose to *"live by faith, not by sight."* [5]

POINTS TO PONDER:

- Before God "disappeared" from your life, what were your preconceptions about his character and the ways he chose to work in others' lives and in yours?
- What did you base these beliefs on? The Bible's doctrines? The teaching you've heard in church or by various Christians?

SUGGESTED ACTION STEP:

Take a half hour to investigate some new sources of information about God, and recheck old sources of your understanding of God's personality, intentions, actions, and revelation methods.

GUIDELINE 10
KEEP A POSITIVE ATTITUDE

One act of thanksgiving, when things go wrong with us, is worth a thousand thanks when things are agreeable to our inclinations.

Saint John of Avila

NEGATIVE AND DESTRUCTIVE THOUGHTS COME NATURALLY DURING A season of dashed hope. Resist the urge to simmer in negativity—work on cultivating and maintaining a positive outlook.

THE POWER OF ATTITUDE

Many of the world's great minds believed in the power of attitude. Sun Tzu, author of *The Art of War*, wrote, "Victorious warriors win first with their minds, and then go to war. Defeated warriors go to war first and then seek to win." Blind poet John Milton wrote, "The mind is its own place, and in itself can make a heaven of hell, and a hell of heaven." And Edwin Cole says, "You don't drown by falling in the water; you drown by *staying* there."

As these thinkers point out, negative attitudes can lead to corrosive consequences. You may not be fighting a war, but perhaps you'll develop more personal fallout, such as a biting cynicism, a soured outlook, a quick-fused temper, an overwhelming anxiety, or decreased productivity unless you can develop some creative coping tools.

Left unchecked, resentment, self-pity, and fear will escalate quickly These harmful emotions can rapidly speed out of control and turn into a fatal avalanche of ruined relationships and other collateral damage.

On the other hand, a constructive mind set can make a positive difference in almost any situation. An optimistic attitude can prevent you from being dragged down by resentment and cynicism. And it can keep you from getting caught up in the vicious cycle of blaming others for your ruined goals.

Positive thinking can open you to new ideas and fresh opportunities. Being upbeat will help you once again appreciate the little things in life. A positive outlook can inspire you to love yourself in more healthy ways that will eliminate or lessen the time you spend beating up on yourself. Developing constructive thoughts about your trauma doesn't mean you negate or minimize your loss. It simply enables you to better cope with it.

You can turn failures into successes. California preacher, Robert Schuller said, "Failure doesn't mean God's abandoned you. It means God has a better idea."

Former two-time heavyweight boxing champion Floyd Patterson was once asked, "Do you know you've been knocked down more times than any other boxer in history?" Patterson gently, but confidently, answered, "Yes, but I got up more times than anyone."

Patterson's response resonated with me on many levels. In college, as a Golden Gloves boxer, I'd been knocked down, but never knocked out. I'd always come back and defeated my opponent. In a similar way,

I had risen above some very tough circumstances in childhood and adulthood. This never-give-up mentality is an attitude that is useful all through life.

SUGGESTIONS FOR KEEPING A POSITIVE ATTITUDE

At first, I had trouble staying positive. Memories haunted me relentlessly. I couldn't "positive think" my way out of the constant negative replays. I knew that the longer I dwelled on all the unfairness I'd experienced, the more my thoughts would sour me, so I finally took action. The following are a few approaches that worked for me and others. Why not experiment with some of them yourself?

Regularly Monitor Your Attitudes, Emotions, and Self-Talk

If your destroyed expectation is recent, it will likely take a constant mental effort to stay focused on positive thoughts. You will need to force yourself, sometimes hour by hour or even minute by minute, to remain mindful of your blessings.

One day, I jotted down a simple poem to remind myself of the importance of attitude:

An Ode to Three Lemons
You pucker and squint
At the slightest hint
Of a lemon's bitter taste.
So why not throw it in the waste?
Life deals its harsh lemons, as well,
Till you feel like you're going through earth's hell.
Better to make lemon meringue pie,
Than constantly bitch, moan, and cry.

This yellow-white pastry, oh so bittersweet
Will brighten your smile as you smack and eat.
Whenever you feel hurt or misunderstood,
Remember the lemon, and make it into
Something bittersweet good.

Jim Stout, novice pie-maker

Do Something, Anything, to Distract Your Harmful Thinking

Experiment with something that will take your mind off the thoughts that besiege you. I tried numerous coping strategies to escape my mental replays of past upsets. What worked one time didn't always work every time, so I had to have a number of survival tactics ready to use. Here are a few ideas you might try:

- Do something, anything, that is *constructive*: finish a house chore, practice a hobby, take a walk, or get some exercise.
- Do something, anything, that is *helpful* for someone else: run an errand for somebody or give encouragement via a phone call, email, text, card, letter, or gift.
- Do something, anything, that *soothes* you: listen to relaxing music, soak in a hot bath, get a pedicure, or watch a sporting event.
- Do something, anything, that *distracts* your obsessive thinking: watch a television show or video, see a movie, golf, garden, or work on a crossword puzzle.

Keep the Big Picture in Mind

Like golf, life is all about recovering! Every golfer—amateur and pro—constantly faces challenges: sand traps, water hazards, trees, wind, out-of-bounds shots, and other obstacles. The trick is to keep moving forward, despite the adversity, with the end goal in mind.

When you are experiencing a mini hell, it's easy to lose sight of your purpose. Living a fulfilled, balanced life means making a lifetime of adjustments. The trick is handling the mental game of dealing with life's guaranteed detours and roadblocks.

Renowned Quaker theologian Dr. Elton Trueblood taught that "the Christian life is a series of new beginnings." During my long, trying situation, I forced myself to often reflect that life is all about recovery from adversities. It's about being willing to start over and over after defeats, losses, failures . . . and even successes.

POINTS TO PONDER:

- Have my spouse, family, or friends made any comments on my negativity?
- How frequently am I watching reruns of my past wounds?

SUGGESTED ACTION STEP:

Take a sheet of paper and list the bad things that have happened due to your destroyed dreams. Then make a list of any good things that could happen as a result of your losses.

GUIDELINE 11
BELIEVE GOD WANTS TO HELP YOU

Though you made me see troubles, many and bitter,
you will restore my life again . . . You will increase my
honor and comfort me once more.

Psalms 71:20–21

GOD TRULY WANTS TO HELP YOU, AND HE WILL GUIDE YOU THROUGH this process. Take heart that *"he tends his flock like a shepherd: He gathers the lambs in his arms and carries them close to his heart; he gently leads those that have young."*[1]

Often, in the midst of my grappling with God and life's unfairness, I thought back to a poem that had fortified me since I first heard it quoted over the radio while in college.

Its author, Rev. A. M. Overton, was a pastor in Mississippi with a wife and three small children. His wife was pregnant with their fourth child. There were complications during delivery, and both she and her baby died.

During the funeral service, the officiating preacher noticed that Overton was writing something on a piece of paper. After the service, the pastor asked him about it, and Overton handed him the poem he'd just written:

Whom God Chooses (He Maketh No Mistake)

My father's way may twist and turn,
My heart may throb and ache,
But in my soul, I'm glad I know,
He maketh no mistake.

My cherished plans may go astray,
My hopes may fade away,
But still I'll trust my Lord to lead,
For he doth know the way.

Tho' night be dark and it may seem,
That day will never break,
I'll pin my faith, my all in him,
He maketh no mistake.

There's so much now I cannot see,
My eyesight's far too dim.
But come what may, I'll simply trust,
And leave it all to him.

For by and by the mist will lift,
And plain it all he'll make,
Through all the way, tho' dark to me,
He made not one mistake. [2]

During my faith trial, Overton's words kept coming back to me, just as they had countless times since my college days. This poem has fortified me to accept God's mysterious, benevolent ways. I've had to constantly remind myself that God is in control, that he alone can see the big picture, and that he is working *with* me, not *against* me.

I knew that without God, life would no longer be meaningful or bearable. I decided that although I couldn't understand God's seeming abandonment and betrayal, I wouldn't walk away from him.

I know I'm not the only person to struggle with this. I recalled many conversations with others who'd faced similar faith wounds. Some people had jettisoned their faith altogether. Some had settled for vague truces with God. And some had managed to use their struggles to renew their faith into a vibrant relationship with God.

If you are experiencing a painful test, feeling what someone once described as a "maximum disorientation," you'll probably be faced with making a choice every step of the way: "Do I give up, quit, and harden with cynicism, or do I trust God in the darkness?" In what direction are you choosing to go right now?

POINTS TO PONDER:

- Can you allow the possibility that God really has your best interests at heart?
- Are you willing to start affirming that God really does want the best for you? Even if it might mean you'll still endure dashed hopes, broken plans, and seemingly wasted efforts?

SUGGESTED ACTION STEP:

Take five minutes a day for several days to create mental pictures of your life under God's attention, defense, and management.

GUIDELINE 12
FIND NEW HOPE

*If you don't learn how to flex, you'll
always be bent out of shape!*

Anonymous

JAN EVES, A WIDOW WITH FIVE CHILDREN, NOTED THAT "EVEN IN THE
darkest of circumstances, when life is not what you ordered, you can
learn to begin again." Finding new hope to replace your shattered
expectations can help you overcome your traumatic experiences.

IF ONE HOPE IS GONE, FIND ANOTHER

Fuller Theological Seminary Professor Lewis Smedes weathered many
heartaches. Despite his own sufferings, or perhaps because of them,
Smedes's teachings and writings have lifted the drooping hearts of
untold numbers of people. In his book *Keeping Hope Alive*, Smedes
describes an incident that exploded new ideas in my mind:

> Tammy Kramer was chief of the outpatient AIDS clinic at Los
> Angeles County Hospital. She was watching a young man who
> had come in one morning for his regular dose of medicine. He

sat in tired silence on a high clinic stool while a new doctor at the clinic poked a needle into his arm and, without looking up at his face, asked, "You are aware, aren't you, that you aren't long for this world—a year at most?" The patient stopped at Tammy's desk on his way out, face distorted in pain, and hissed, "That SOB took away my hope." [1]

Smedes reacted to that emotional interchange: "I guess he did. Maybe it's time to find another [hope]." [2] The lesson? If one hope is dashed, you've got to move onto the next.

Having seen some of my own hopes smashed, I certainly understood that patient's desperate, angry reaction. After reading Smedes's story, I decided that I, too, needed to find other hopes to replace the ones I'd lost.

Somewhere, I came across an old cavalry slogan that went something like this: "When your horse dies, dismount and saddle another." I paraphrased those words to apply to my situation, "When your hope dies, let it go and grab another."

RECALL GOD'S PAST INTERVENTIONS

Steve Jobs noted, "You can't connect the dots looking forward; you can only connect them by looking backwards. So you have to trust that the dots will somehow connect in your future." [3]

By looking to the past for patterns of God at work in your life and the lives of others, you can look to the future and know what to expect. Unquestionably, when you are in the midst of any kind of crisis, it's easy to be so inundated with your current problem that spiritual amnesia blots out all remembrances of God's past blessings. But it's crucial to remember them.

Baal Shem Tov, the founder of the Hasidic movement, once said, "Forgetfulness prolongs the exile; remembrance is the secret of redemption."

You can use your memories in one of two ways: one way is *not* helpful, the other can be very helpful.

The first option you have is simply to do what comes naturally in difficult times: constantly recall instant replays of all your hurts and unfair treatment. This will focus your anger at God, concentrating your thoughts on how he has misled you and has orchestrated your broken dreams. This use of your memory can keep you locked into the pains of the past, trapping you in self-pity, bitterness, and cynicism.

The second way you can use your memory will instill you with the hope and endurance to change your focus onto positive things. Fixing your attention on positives means calling to mind the instances when God has acted on your behalf as well as in the lives of people you know. This mental exercise can give you strength to gut it out through your terrible upsets and give you hope that sooner or later things will get better.

The motto of the Simon Wiesenthal Foundation in Los Angeles is "Hope lives when people remember." [4] I've found this to be true—using my memory in constructive ways actually helped my faith become more tenacious. When I chose to think about past instances of God's faithfulness, I was able to persist and wait for him to intervene. I reasoned that if I could be delivered from past traumas before, then I could be rescued again.

Maybe this is why the psalmist penned these verses:

I remember the days of long ago; I meditate on all your works and consider what your hands have done . . . I thirst for you like a parched land. [5]

My soul is downcast within me; therefore I will remember you from the land of the Jordan, the heights of Hermon, from Mount Mizar. [6]

I will remember the deeds of the Lord; yes, I will remember your miracles of long ago. I will consider all your works and meditate on all your mighty deeds ... With your mighty arm you redeemed your people. [7]

VISUALIZE A NEW OUTCOME FOR YOUR LIFE

Visualizing a different outcome for your life, perhaps one you have never considered before, can help you move forward. Lecturer Maria Robinson observed, "Nobody can go back and start a new beginning, but anyone can start today and make a new ending."

In *The Seven Habits of Highly Effective People*, Stephen R. Covey wrote, "Begin with the end in mind." Time and again, Covey's words filled me with hope.When I visualized new outcomes in my life, I had to continually remind myself to stay open to accepting, and then building on, God's "Plan B."

Whenever I started to dwell on my losses, I often came back to a statement by Helen Keller, the famous blind, hearing-impaired writer and activist for the disabled:

When one door of happiness closes, another opens; but often we look so long at the closed door that we do not see the one which has been opened for us. [8]

Fastened on my garage wall is a framed picture by artist Lynn Kessinger. It's a comical but accurate take on the same idea:

When God closes one door
He always opens another,
But it's hell in the hallway!

Keller and Kessinger offered key insights into my faith situation. It hurt being so helpless to change what had happened in my life, but I knew what I had to do: my survival meant that I had to be patient and remain open to letting God reveal a new path for my life.

POINTS TO PONDER:

- Can you recall a time God got involved and helped in your life or that of a family member, relative, or friend?
- Are you willing to picture some positive outcomes from your recent loss?

SUGGESTED ACTION STEP:

As an alternative to concentrating on your defeats, take a few minutes to think of some benefits that can come your way. Write these down, and then discuss them with someone.

GUIDELINE 13
SURRENDER TO GOD

We must be willing to get rid of the life we've planned
so as to have the life that is waiting for us.
Margaret Meade

TO MOVE OUT OF A MARATHON FAITH TRIAL, YOU'LL EVENTUALLY NEED to decide if you're going to turn your life and will over to God's care, protection, and guidance. This kind of surrender means you'll need to resume living by faith and not by sight. It requires letting go of your own strength and grabbing on to God, depending on him for the positive outcome of your situation, your reputation, and your life.

Long ago, I memorized the Bible's definition of faith: "*Confidence in what we hope for and assurance of what we do not see . . . without faith it is impossible to please God, because anyone who comes to him must believe that he exists and that he rewards those who earnestly seek him.*" [1]

I knew that living by faith meant I must hand over even the smallest details of my life to God's sovereign, benevolent direction. I had to trust that God, and God alone, could make good come from bad.

Submitting to God is a deliberate choice. It's an individual matter—only *you alone* can decide to give yourself and your plans to God's leadership.

To *not* make a decision about who is really going to manage your life is, in reality, a decision to manage your own circumstances—simply kicking your life in neutral gear is really a decision to avoid linking up with God.

Maybe you gave yourself to God some time ago. But, because of your losses, you've chosen to take back control of your life and no longer rely on him. Have you thought about whether you or God will be the central director of your life from this point on?

How do you go about raising your white flag of surrender? Maybe you can take a clue from Christina Rossetti, a poet who suffered from physical and mental illness. Her poem "In the Bleak Midwinter," gets to the heart of spiritual surrender:

> What can I give him, poor as I am?
> If I were a shepherd, I would bring a lamb;
> If I were a wise man, I would do my part;
> Yet what can I give him—give him my heart.

In my own faith battle, I finally came to the place where I chose to trust God no matter what, saying, "I'm choosing to depend on you to work in my life, Lord, even though I haven't a clue what you're doing."

Nevertheless, within a day or so of deciding to turn my life and will over to God, anger, doubts, and uncertainties again crept into my thinking, and I had to re-submit myself to him. Whenever negatives started to flood my thoughts, I consciously yielded to God—again and again and again.

As I tried to manage my feelings, a stanza from John Donne's *A Hymn to Christ* struck me in a different but encouraging way:

> Batter my heart, three-person'd God; for you
> As yet but knock, breathe, shine, and seek to mend;
> That I may rise and stand, o'erthrow me, and bend
> Your force to break, blow, burn, and make me new.

A big part of turning my future over to God meant choosing to give up my angry, victim-like thinking. I had to trust that in spite of how bad things looked, God was supervising the events of my life in ways I couldn't comprehend.

GOD WILL BECOME YOUR GUIDE

Long ago, the prophet Isaiah authored these hopeful words: *"Although the Lord gives you the bread of adversity and the water of affliction, your teachers will be hidden no more; with your own eyes you will see them. Whether you turn to the right or to the left, your ears will hear a voice behind you, saying, 'This is the way; walk in it.' "* [2]

The psalmist wrote, *"Your path led through the sea, your way through the mighty waters, though your footprints were not seen."* [3]

I reminded myself of God's commitment to bless me for trusting him:

> *Blessed is the one who perseveres under trial because, having stood the test, that person will receive the crown of life that the Lord has promised to those who love him.* [4]

> *I will lead the blind by ways they have not known, along unfamiliar paths I will guide them; I will turn the darkness into light before*

them and make the rough places smooth. These are the things I will do; I will not forsake them. [5]

In the midst of my misery, and in order to boost my faith in God's guidance, I often read the final stanza from William Cullen Bryant's "Ode to a Waterfowl":

He, who, from zone to zone,
Guides through the boundless sky thy certain flight,
In the long way that I must tread alone,
Will lead my steps aright.

SOMETIMES YOU'VE GOT TO WAIT

Sometimes handing a situation over to God means to stop working and simply wait for him to act. I had a tough time with this—it was scary not knowing what was ahead. But I had to be willing to live with uncertainty and count on God's positive plan for me in the process.

All I could do was follow the example of the Apostle Paul when he was trapped in a life-threatening storm at sea. After trying their best to stabilize their ship, Paul and his shipmates eventually chose to drop the sea anchor and hunker down, simply riding the storm out. [6]

King David must have been trudging through similar circumstances when he wrote, *"Have mercy on me, my God . . . for in you I take refuge. I will take refuge in the shadow of your wings until the disaster has passed."* [7]

It felt good to finally "let go and let God." Peace that had eluded me for so long began its return.

POINTS TO PONDER:

- Are you willing to imagine both the good and bad effects of your present (and future) circumstances? And are you willing to turn them over to God?
- Are you ready to release your future hopes to God?

SUGGESTED ACTION STEP:

Tell God that you want to trust him with a specific plan, then make a deliberate choice to leave the results, good or bad, to him.

GUIDELINE 14
REVIEW AND REVISE YOUR LIFE GOALS FREQUENTLY

When it's obvious that a goal cannot be reached,
don't adjust the goal, adjust the action steps.

Chinese proverb

ANY SIGNIFICANT ACHIEVEMENT IN LIFE REQUIRES A GREAT DEAL OF determination to meet your goals without letting barriers stop you. Poet Langston Hughes describes the importance of tenacity:

Hold fast to dreams.
For if dreams die,
Life is a broken-winged bird,
That cannot fly.
Hold fast to dreams.
For when dreams go,
Life is a barren field,
Frozen with snow. [1]

As Hughes so eloquently states, you've got to hold on tight when the going gets rough. Resolve, dedication, discipline, perseverance, grit, and determination are key to achieving anything. Yet, in spite of all your resolve and hard work, life sometimes throws such huge obstructions that achieving your original goals becomes impossible.

For example, a pro football player may work for years to perfect his talent in order to fulfill his dream of becoming a Hall-of-Fame player. But it takes only one bad hit to result in a brain, neck, or knee injury that permanently disables him from playing.

That player must then choose to either react with bitterness and despair, or to grieve his lost dream, flex, and move on to another career path. Sadly, some players have worked so hard, and are so fixed on their goal, that when a tragic injury wipes out their plans, they collapse into defeatism.

FAILED DREAMS CAN LEAD TO BETTER THINGS

Writer Caroline Myss observed, "Many of our life crises are divinely scheduled to get us to change and head in a different direction."

Although clinging to your dreams and working harder and harder to fulfill them may seem noble, it can also make you blind to other possibilities.

Dr. Maribeth Ekey offers a helpful option for dealing with dashed dreams: "Despair can open us to mourning, letting go and trying life from new angles." [2] And songwriter Paul Abram Constantine emphasizes that "dreams are never destroyed, only rearranged." [3]

Input from Ekey, Constantine, and others helped me open up to other possible projects that could use my experiences and skills. I found myself asking, "How would my Christian role models get through this? In what ways can I use the pain I've been through to benefit others?"

I wondered, "What's God trying to teach me through this? Should I restart my efforts and keep forging ahead on this project? Or should I quit fighting and simply accept this closed door as a 'no' from God? Has he shut these doors so I'll enter others that he's preparing for me?"

Eventually you may find that you are once again thinking of checking out new opportunities. This is an indicator that God may be leading you out of your seclusion and back on to solid ground. In time, your new life will emerge from the ashes of your disappointments. Therefore, as you can, try making new goals and plans. But stay flexible and revise them as necessary.

TAKE THE INITIATIVE TO MEET YOUR GOALS

Once I had reviewed and revised my goals, I knew I had to start doing something about them. I had been praying, but taking no focused action, until one day I remembered that an addict had told me, "Prayer without some kind of action is only a wish." Similarly, Walt Disney quipped, "The way to get started is to quit talking and begin doing."

This was certainly true in my faith struggle. I knew I had to do more than just hope and pray for a new project. I needed to take some concrete steps. Slowly, I sensed a new direction to go. I kept listening for God to clarify his actions, and even though I lacked any explanations from him, I decided to move ahead with my life. I concluded that if I were to escape my bitter circumstances and obtain God's blessings, I'd need to initiate some key changes:

- Make extra efforts to maintain close contact with God
- Reframe my various "failed" projects
- Mend relationships with certain people
- Reprioritize my use of time

- Start additional projects
- Remain open to God's opportunities to use my skills and experiences, such as speaking, writing, counseling, and consulting

I worked at nourishing my fragile, newly-rebuilt trust that God was working in my life. The words of books, articles, songs, and hymns took root. They slowly lifted me above my previous hard blows, lit a candle of hope, and ignited a desire to start over. I looked at my options and began setting new goals and developing new plans.

Then, one uneventful day, seemingly for no particular reason, I started to feel hopeful about the future. Little by little, my hopelessness started to drain away, and in its place a new optimism slowly seeped in. It was like the dense fog had finally started to lift and I could see patches of clear blue sky. In my newfound outlook, I shouted inwardly:

God, if you have some new assignments for me, I'm willing to take them on. Please show me what you want me to do. I'll watch for your confirmations that I'm doing the right thing, just like I did before. And I'll work just as hard to complete them.

Only this time, I'll hold on to them loosely. If there are setbacks, dead ends, or other difficulties, I'll give it my best efforts, but I'll let you determine the results. I'll let go of my expectations for the project, and turn the details, deadlines, and end product over to your supervision.

That week, I began working on the book I'd started nearly a year earlier. I started doing devotional time again, and on the second day of writing, I came across a startling statement from *The Message*, a paraphrase of the Bible:

The best thing you can do right now is to finish what you started last year and not let those good intentions grow stale. . . . You've got what it takes to finish it up, so go to it. Once the commitment is clear, you do what you can, not what you can't. The heart regulates the hands. [4]

Talk about clear reassurance to return to my writing efforts! I felt as though God was speaking directly to me, and this book is the direct result of following those renewed efforts.

POINTS TO PONDER:

- Are you open to setting new goals and making backup plans?
- How will this change the way you prioritize your time use, relationships, and projects?

SUGGESTED ACTION STEP:

Take ten minutes to mentally reframe your losses, then take ten more minutes to write about your newly conceived outcomes.

GUIDELINE 15
KEEP MOVING FORWARD

The greatest thing in this world is not so much where
we are, but in which direction we are moving.

Oliver Wendell Holmes

ON SEPTEMBER 7, 1892, JAMES J. CORBETT WON THE FIRST HEAVYWEIGHT championship prizefight in which the contestants used boxing gloves. Corbett won by knocking out John L. Sullivan in the twenty-first round. Not only a great athlete, Corbett also had a way with words. When asked why he'd been so successful as a boxer, he replied:

Fight one more round. When your feet are so tired that you have to shuffle back to the center of the ring, fight one more round. When your arms are so tired that you can hardly lift your hands to come on guard, fight one more round. When your nose is bleeding and your eyes are black and you are so tired you wish your opponent would crack you one on the jaw and put you to sleep, fight one more round—remembering that the man who always fights one more round is never whipped. [1]

A hard fact of life is that one of the best ways to get through difficulties is simply to endure them. British prime minister Winston Churchill, no stranger to inner battles, advised, "Success consists of going from failure to failure without loss of enthusiasm . . . If you're going through hell, keep going . . . Never give up. Never give up. Never give up!"

There are numerous ways people give up and stay stuck where they are. For some, there is a strong temptation to avoid dealing with a faith-trying episode by minimizing its seriousness: "My problems may seem bad, but many others have it far worse." Others rationalize, "I'll be okay with these reversals. My core faith won't be affected." A huge number of believers numb their disappointments by excess work, ministry activities, food, alcohol, drugs, or other means.

Christ-followers who've found the hope and courage to continue moving forward do so by doing three things:

- They work hard to frequently recall God's interventions in their pasts.
- They dare to believe that God will continue to work in them for their well being, the best interests of others, and his purposes.
- They move ahead, despite their losses, relying on God to sustain, guide, and bless them.

I've done all these. But I'm realistic enough to know that, sooner or later, another faith-test will confront me—that's life. Dave Dravecky writes, "Rebuilding a shattered perspective is not a one-time deal!" [2] This certainly has been true for me. That's why my frequent prayer is:

Lord, help me never underestimate what you can do with the most unlikely of circumstances. Thank you for loving me and using my frustrations, failures, doubts, and gifts for your purposes. Give me the strength to hold on and the joy of seeing things through to completion for your glory.

I admit that there's a great temptation for me to continue holding on to my past. But if I do, it will only keep me from moving forward. We should live like the Apostle Paul, who said, *"Forgetting what is behind and straining toward what is ahead, I press on toward the goal."* [3]

Even during those times when I'm able to let go of my past, occasionally I still feel overwhelmed and I'm tempted to give up on a stalled project. When this happens, I lean on these life-lifting words: *"No temptation has overtaken you except what is common to mankind. And God is faithful; he will not let you be tempted beyond what you can bear. But when you are tempted, he will also provide a way out so that you can endure it."* [4]

Although you may be tempted to give up, remind youself that overcoming your struggle will take time. And always remember that if you just keep fighting one more round, you'll triumph in the end.

POINTS TO PONDER:

- What hurdles do you face in your process of healing and rebuilding?
- Are you open to using new ways of dealing with interruptions, obstacles, or failures?

SUGGESTED ACTION STEP:

This week, amp up your efforts to cope with at least one faith stumbling block.

CONCLUSION

FROM ONE FAITH STRUGGLER TO ANOTHER: WHETHER OR NOT YOU FEEL God's presence, I encourage you to hang on for one more week. Use whatever it takes to keep from sinking. Fight one more round. Don't stop searching. Keep moving. And try reflecting on the prayerful words from Lord Tennyson, from his poem "In Memorium":

> Be near me when my light is low,
> When the blood creeps, and the nerves prick
> And tingle; and the heart is sick,
> And all the wheels of being slow.
> Be near me when the sensuous frame
> Is racked with pangs that conquer trust;
> And Time, a manic scattering dust.
> And life, a fury slinging flame.
> Be near me when my faith is dry,
> And men the flies of latter spring,
> That lay their eggs, and sting and sing
> And weave their petty cells and die.
> Be near me when I fade away.
> To point the term of human strife,
> And on the low dark verge of life
> The Twilight of eternal day.

Even if you still don't feel God's presence, even if you still feel betrayed, I hope that in the midst of your spiritual battle you will be heartened by these awesome promises from the Bible:

Do not fear . . . do not let your hands hang limp. The Lord your God is with you, the Mighty Warrior who saves. He will take great delight in you. In his love he will no longer rebuke you, but will rejoice over you with singing. [1]

So do not fear, for I am with you; do not be dismayed, for I am your God. I will strengthen you and help you; I will uphold you with my righteous right hand. [2]

Forget the former things; do not dwell on the past. See, I am doing a new thing! Now it springs up; do you not perceive it? I am making a way in the wilderness and streams in the wasteland. [3]

As you reflect upon those verses, think about the words of this beautiful prayer from Saint John of Avila: "I pray God may open your eyes and let you see what hidden treasures he bestows on us in the trials from which the world thinks only to flee."

EPILOGUE

THANKS TO MY SPIRITUAL BREAKDOWN, MY MINISTRY HAS ACTUALLY expanded and taken on a deeper dimension, giving me a greater motivation to share the experiences of my spiritually bleak times.

This desire has spilled over to influence my writing and speaking. In addition, a large chunk of my time has involved counseling that deals with career guidance and clergy issues. I also consult on mental illness recovery and related topics with churches, colleges, seminaries, hospitals, and other organizations. All of these pursuits have been influenced by my life experiences, especially regarding my relationship with God.

Yes, the painful memories of my faith meltdown still remain, sensitive and easily triggered. But I won't wait until those scars have fully healed to make positive use of them. The last stanza from songwriter Leonard Cohen's song "Anthem" beautifully illustrates my feelings about reaching out to others who hurt, even while you yourself are still healing:

> Ring the bells that can still ring
> Forget your perfect offering
> There is a crack, a crack in everything
> That's how the light gets in
> That's how the light gets in
> That's how the light gets in.[1]

On top of this, even in the midst of occasional doubts, questions, and sense of God's absence, I moved ahead to undertake some new, exciting opportunities. These include, among other things, finishing twelve years of writing projects and over a dozen books, including the one you're reading here.

What I've done with all my limitations, you can do even better in your own way—and succeed far greater than you can imagine. Now it's your turn to rebuild, to move out. And as you launch into a new chapter of your life, may God bless you!

I'll leave you with this: Mark Twain, the author and humorist, is said to have written these inspiring lines, "Twenty years from now you will be more disappointed by the things you *didn't* do than by the ones you *did* do. So throw off the bowlines. Sail away from the safe harbor. Catch the trade winds in your sails. Explore. Dream. Discover."

ACKNOWLEDGMENTS

ABOVE ALL, I THANK GOD, MY WONDERFUL COUNSELOR AND GREAT Shepherd, who patiently put up with my spiritual meltdowns, and sent quiet support through people and information to reassure me in the midst of my bleakest times. I'm exceedingly thankful that he never let me go, and that he has given me strength to start over and over and over.

I am also grateful to the following people for their help in making this book possible:

- My psychologist, who counseled, consoled, and guided me during some of my rough patches: Dr. Laurel Basbas
- My friends who listened to my faith struggles and shared their insights and encouragement: Lucky and Penny Arnold, Connie Bean, Larry and Sue Ann Beaty, John Chandler, Dr. Gunnar and Susan Christiansen, Gex Coons, Dr. Dick and June Cooper, Dick and Cathy Dowell, Ellen Enochs, Jeff Fryer, Fred and Joan Hearn, Ron and Catherine Hilliard, Cliff Ishigaki, Bob and Joan Johnson, Dr. Gregory Katz, Jack and May Kline, Jim Kok, Bill and Annie Lightcap, Bob and Marilyn Long, Scott and Carolyn McOwen, Bob Numrich, Ozzie and Cleo Purdy, Vince Roman, Dr. Himasiri De Silva, Ken Stokes, Jake and Alice Swartout, Tom Taillon, Bill and Chris Tassio, Scott and Patti Thompson, Hank and Margaret Weber, and others
- My editors, who gave valuable shaping and guidance in manuscript details: Andrew Kroeger and Stephanie Starr. I'm indebted for

what I've learned from them, and for their support, patience, and encouragement through the lengthy writing process

- My copyeditors and proofreaders, who corrected grammar and typographic flaws: Shelley Atwood, Sharon Young, Janelle Killingsworth, Julie Lopes, and Elijah Dove
- My office helpers, who copied, collated, stapled, and filed articles used in the research and production of this book: Stephen Reese, Lisa Waldschmidt, and Robert Langdale
- My computer technicians, who installed programs, fixed computer glitches, and taught me, the ultimate computer-challenged writer, how to survive in the techie world and not lose my sanity in the process: Mike Adler and Taylor Allee
- My permissions researchers, for tracking down contacts: Sean Fernald, Susan Lessick, and Rebecca Trinklein
- My typist, who saved me much time and untold typos: Lyssa Eschel
- My friend who rented her Big Bear home to me at a modest rate so that I could write there, undistracted: Ginny Okamoto

RESOURCES

SUFFERING AND LIFE'S UNFAIRNESS

Bainton, Roland H. *Here I Stand*. New York and Nashville, TN: Abington Press, 1950.

Camus, Albert. *The Fall*. French-The Fall [*La Chute*]. New York: Vintage Books (Random House), 1956.

Camus, Albert. *The Myth of Sisyphus*. New York: Vintage Books (Random House), 1942.

Camus, Albert. *The Plague*. New York: Gallimard Librairie (Alfred A. Knopf), 1948.

Camus, Albert. *The Stranger*. [*The Outsider*, (L'Étranger)]. New York: Gallimard Librairie (Alfred A. Knopf), 1942.

Chambers, Oswald. *The Complete Works of Oswald Chambers*. (Baffled to Fight Better; Job & the Problem of Suffering). Grand Rapids, MI: Discovery House Publishers and RBC Ministries, 2000.

Cloud, Henry Ph.D. and Townsend, Ph.D. *12 Christian Beliefs that Can Drive You Crazy; Relief from False Assumptions*. Grand Rapids, MI: Zondervan Publishing House, 1994.

Frankl, Victor E. *Man's Search for Meaning*. New York: Pocket Books, 1959.

Lewis, C.S. *God in the Dock: Essays on Theology and Ethics*. Grand Rapids, MI: William B. Eerdmans Publishing Company, 1970.

Lewis, C.S. *The Great Divorce*. Westbury, United Kingdom: HarperOne, Geoffrey Bles, 1945.

Lewis, C.S., Ph. D. *A Grief Observed*. San Francisco: Harper, 1964.

Lewis, C.S. *Mere Christianity*. San Francisco: Harper, 1952.

Lewis, C.S. *The Problem of Pain*. New York: HarperCollins, 1940.

Kafka, Franz. *The Metamorphosis*. (Original Title: *Die Verwandlung*). Austria-Hungary: Kurt Wolff Verlag Leipzig, 1915.

Kafka, Franz. *The Trial: The Complete Stories*. London: Minerva, 1983.

Kushner, Harold S. *When Bad Things Happen to Good People*. New York: Avon Books, 1981.

Lobdell, William. "Losing My Religion: How I Lost My Faith Reporting on Religion in America—and Found Unexpected Peace." New York: HarperCollins, 2009.

Phillips, J. B. "Your God Is Too Small: A Guide for Believers and Skeptics Alike." New York: Touchstone, 1952.

Russell, Bertrand. "Why I Am Not a Christian: And Other Essays on Religion and Related Subjects." New York: Touchstone, 1967.

Sartre, Jean-Paul. *The Age of Reason*. Translator: Eric Sutton, Gallimard. New York: Knopf, Vintage, 1945.

Sartre, Jean-Paul. *No Exit*. French Play, 1944.

Smedes, Lewis B., Ph.d. "How Can It Be All Right When Everything Is All Wrong?" New York: Pocket Books, 1982.

Smedes, Lewis B., Ph.D. *Keeping Hope Alive*. Nashville, TN: Thomas Nelson Publishers, 1998.

Tolstoy, Leo. *A Confession and Other Religious Writings*. New York: Penguin Books, 1987.

Tolstoy, Leo. *Resurrection*. New York: Grosset & Dunlap Publishers, 1899.

Wolff, Pierre, *May I Hate God?* New York/Ramsey/Toronto: Paulist Press, 1979.

Yancey, Philip. *Disappointment with God*. Grand Rapids, MI: Zondervan Publishing House, 1988.

Yancey, Philip. *The Question that Never Goes Away: Why?* Grand Rapids, MI: Zondervan Publishing House, 2014

Yancey, Phillip. *Where Is God When It Hurts?* Grand Rapids, MI: Zondervan Publishing House, 1977.

DEPRESSION

Cronkite, Kathy. *On the Edge of Darkness.* New York: Doubleday, 1994.

Greene-McCreight, Kathryn. "Darkness Is My Only Companion: A Christian Response to Mental Illness." Grand Rapids, MI: Brazos Press, 2006.

Hart, Archibald D., Ph.D. *Unmasking Male Depression.* Nashville, TN: W Publishing Group, 2001.

Hart, Archibald D., Ph.D and Weber, Catherine Hart, Ph.D. *Unveiling Depression in Women.* Grand Rapids, MI: Fleming H. Ravelle, 2002.

Skoglund, Elizabeth Ruth. *Bright Days and Dark Nights with Charles Spurgeon.* Grand Rapids, MI: Baker Books, 2000.

Yapko, Michael D., Ph.D. *Breaking the Patterns of Depression.* New York: Doubleday, 1997.

PRACTICAL HELP

Carlson, Dwight L. "Why Do Christians Shoot Their Wounded? Helping (Not Hurting) Those with Emotional Difficulties." Downers Grove, IL: InterVarsityPress, 1994.

Cloud, Henry, Ph.D and Townsend, John, Ph.D. *Boundaries.* Grand Rapids, MI: Zondervan Publishing House, 1992.

Cloud, Henry, Ph.D. and Townsend, John, Ph.D. *Changes that Heal.* Grand Rapids, MI: Zondervan Publishing House, 1993.

Cloud, Henry, Ph.D. *Necessary Endings.* New York, NY: HarperCollins, 2011

Ekey, Maribeth, Psy.D. "Shattered Hopes Renewed Hearts: What to Do with Wishes that Don't Come True." Ann Arbor, MI: Servant Publications, 1998.

Leadership Journal, "Dark Nights of the Soul." Marshall Shelley, editor-in-chief. Carol Stream, IL: Christianity Today Publisher, Fall 2011.

Mason, John. "Don't Wait for Your Ship to Come in . . . Swim Out to Meet It!" Tulsa, OK: Honor Books, 1994.

Schlessinger, Laura, Ph.D. *Bad Childhood—Good Life.* New York: HarperCollins, 2006.

Schuller, Robert H. *Life's Not Fair, but God Is Good.* New York: Bantam Books, 1993.

Schuller, Robert H., *Tough Times Never Last, but Tough People Do.* New York: Bantam Books, 1984.

Schuller, Robert H. *Turning Hurts into Halos.* Nashville, TN: Thomas Nelson Publishers, 1995.

Schuller, Robert A. *What Happens to Good People When Bad Things Happen*. Grand Rapids, MI: Fleming H. Revell, 1995.

Seligman, Martin E.P. Ph.D. *Learned Optimism*. New York: Pocket Books, 1990.

Siebert, Al, Ph.D. *The Survivor Personality*. New York: The Berkley Publishing Company, 1993.

Smedes, Lewis B., Ph.D. *Forgive & Forget: Healing the Hurts We Don't Deserve*. New York: HarperOne, 1984.

Stearns, Ann Kaiser. *Living Through Personal Crisis*. New York: Ballantine Books, 1984.

Stoltz, Paul G, Ph.D. *Adversity Quotient*. New York: John Wiley & Sons, Inc., 1997.

Wright, Norman H, Ph.D. *Resilience: Rebounding When Life's Upsets Knock You Down*. Ann Arbor, MI: Servant Publications, 1997.

Yancey, Philip. *Disappointment with God*. Grand Rapids, MI: Zondervan Publishing House, 1992.

Yancey, Philip. "Soul Survivor (How Thirteen Unlikely Mentors Helped My Faith Survive the Church)." New York: Random House, Inc., 2003.

Yancey, Philip. *Where Is God When It Hurts?* Grand Rapids, MI: Zondervan Publishing House, 1990.

Christian Formation and Direction Ministries; *cfdm.org*

Spiritual Directors International; *sdiworld.org*

Stillpoint: The Center for Christian Spirituality; *stillpointca.org*

NOTES

PREFACE

1. Proverbs 24:32

INTRODUCTION

1. *Leadership Journal,* Fall 2011

CHAPTER 1

1. Isaiah 39:8
2. Matthew 5:45
3. Isaiah 55:9
4. Job 23:2
5. Numbers 11:11
6. Psalms 43:2
7. Job 30:26–27
8. *Keeping Hope Alive,* by Dr. Lewis Smedes
9. *Webster's New World College Dictionary,* 3rd Edition
10. Hebrews 13:5
11. Psalms 46:1
12. Psalms 139:7–8
13. Psalms 22:1
14. Psalms 13:1–2; Psalms 80:14
15. Job 13:24
16. Job 7:11
17. Job 14:19
18. Job 19:8, 10–11
19. Jeremiah 20:7
20. Lamentations 3:2–3, 5, 8, 17–18
21. Judges 6:13
22. Ruth 1:20
23. Matthew 27:46
24. Matthew 17:22

CHAPTER 2

1. Isaiah 40:27
2. Isaiah 45:15
3. Isaiah 49:14
4. *A Grief Observed,* by C.S. Lewis
5. Isaiah 54:7–8, 10
6. "For The Mountains Shall Depart," by Hank Beebe (composer), Drinda Frenzel (vocalist), Steven Applegate (arranger)
7. Jeremiah 29:13–14
8. Job 30:25–27

CHAPTER 3

1. Psalms 46:1
2. Jeremiah 45:3
3. Romans 9:2
4. *A Grief Observed,* by C. S. Lewis
5. 2 Chronicles 32:31
6. Lamentations 3:33
7. 1 Samuel 16:14, 23
8. Psalms 106:14–15, 24–25

CHAPTER 4

1. *Alcoholic's Anonymous; The Big Book, 4th edition,* pages 64, 66, 145
2. Psalms 55:2; Psalms 77:1–4
3. Romans 8:28
4. Sister Madeleva Williams
5. John 15:2 (emphasis added)
6. Deuteronomy 32:10–12

CHAPTER 5

1. Luke 17:1
2. James 1:2–4
3. *Four Quartets: The Little Gidding,* by T. S. Eliot
4. Jeremiah 7:13, 15, 29
5. Jeremiah 31:34
6. Proverbs 3:5

7. Isaiah 42:16

CHAPTER 6

1. Isaiah 38:17
2. Psalms 40:2
3. "Learned Optimism: How to Change Your Mind and Your Life,"
    by Dr. Martin Seligman.
4. 2 Corinthians 1:3–4

GUIDELINE 1

1. *Abide with Me*, by Henry Francis Lyte
2. Psalms 88:14
3. *Here I Stand*, by Roland Bainton
4. Ibid.
5. Ibid.

GUIDELINE 2

1. *Newsweek*, May 7, 2007, copyright 2007
2. *Keeping Hope Alive*, by Dr. Lewis Smedes
3. *Mother Teresa: Come Be My Light; The Private Writings of the
    Saint of Calcutta*
4. Los Angeles Times, "Facing Tragedy, Pastors Put Their Faith on
    Hold," by Claire Luna

GUIDELINE 3

1. "Shattered Hopes, Renewed Hearts," by Mary Beth Ekey, Psy.D.
2. *The Collected Poems*, by Elizabeth Jennings
3. John 11:35
4. Matthew 26:38
5. Isaiah 53:3
6. Matthew 5:4
7. Ecclesiastes 3:4
8. 1 Thessalonians 4:13
9. *Unmasking Male Depression*, by Dr. Archibald Hart
10. Ephesians 5:6–7

GUIDELINE 4

1. *Alcoholic's Anonymous; The Big Book,* 4th edition, page 417

GUIDELINE 5

1. Hebrews 10:24–25
2. Ecclesiastes 4:9–12
3. Proverbs 25:20
4. Psalms 38:11
5. Psalms 69:20
6. Job 19:13–15, 19
7. *To Bedlam and Part Way Back,* by Anne Sexton
8. Job 4:7–8
9. Macbeth, IV, 3
10. Proverbs 1:5
11. Proverbs 20:18
12. Proverbs 12:15
13. Proverbs 24:6
14. Proverbs 15:22

GUIDELINE 6

1. Jeremiah 33:3
2. Luke 18:1
3. 1 Peter 5:7
4. James 4:2
5. Psalms 142:1–2
6. Psalms 86:16–17
7. Psalms 139:13, 16
8. Isaiah 58:11
9. Isaiah 43:1–2
10. Hebrews 13:5
11. Isaiah 43:18–19
12. Romans 8:38–39
13. Isaiah 43:5
14. Matthew 28:20
15. Psalms 121:3–4, 7–8
16. Romans 8:26–27

17. Romans 8:34–35

1. 1 Corinthians 14:20
2. Luke 11:9
3. Proverbs 14:15
4. Matthew 22:37 (emphasis added)
5. Isaiah 55:8–9
6. John 13:7 (emphasis added)

1. 1 Thessalonians 1:2–3 (J. B. Phillips Translation) (emphasis added)
2. 1 Peter 4:12–13
3. Ephesians 4:23
4. Proverbs 15:15
5. Philippians 4:8
6. Psalms 145:14
7. Philippians 3:8
8. James 1:12
9. Isaiah 49:15–16
10. Psalms 34:18
11. Jeremiah 29:11
12. *Pray, Praise, and Promises*, by Warren W. Wiersbe
13. 1 Peter 1:6–7
14. Genesis 28:16

1. Catechism of the Catholic Church, Second Edition, Chapter Two: The Sacraments of Healing; Article 5
2. Isaiah 48:10, 17
3. 1 Kings 8:12
4. Jeremiah 23:23–24
5. 2 Corinthians 5:7

GUIDELINE 11

1. Isaiah 40:11
2. *Whom God Chooses,* by A. M. Overton

GUIDELINE 12

1. *Keeping Hope Alive,* by Dr. Lewis Smedes
2. Ibid.
3. *iCon Steve Jobs, the Greatest Second Act in the History of Business,* by Jeffrey S. Young and William L. Simon
4. Simon Wiesenthal Foundation
5. Psalms 143:3–6
6. Psalms 42:6
7. Psalms 77:11–12, 15
8. *We Bereaved,* 1929, *To Love this Life,* 1928, by Helen Keller

GUIDELINE 13

1. Hebrews 11:1, 6
2. Isaiah 30:20–21
3. Psalms 77:19
4. James 1:12
5. Isaiah 42:16
6. Acts 27:17
7. Psalms 57:1

GUIDELINE 14

1. "Dreams," from *The Collected Poems of Langston Hughes*
2. *Shattered Hopes, Renewed Hearts,* by Mary Beth Ekey
3. Paul Abram Constantine
4. 2 Corinthians 8:11–14 (The Message)

GUIDELINE 15

1. James J. Corbett
2. David Dravecky
3. Philippians 3:13–14
4. 1 Corinthians 10:13

CONCLUSION

1. Zephaniah 3:16–17
2. Isaiah 41:10
3. Isaiah 43:18–19

EPILOGUE

1. *Anthem, from Stranger Music: Selected Poems and Songs,* by Leonard Cohen

PERMISSIONS

I gratefully acknowledge and appreciate the following permissions granted:

Paul Abram Constantine. Used with permission.

Print by Sister M. Madeleva. Used with permission.

Rev. A. M. Overton. *Whom God Chooses.* Used with permission from Rob Overton.

Roland Bainton. *Here I Stand: A Life of Martin Luther.* Copyright© 2012, Used with permission from Forgotten Books.

Simon Wiesenthal. *Hope Lives When People Remember.* Used with permission, courtesy of Simon Wiesenthal Center.

Song placed on www.drjimstout.com: "For The Mountains Shall Depart", Hank Beebe (composer), Drinda Frenzel (vocalist), Steven Applegate (arranger).

The brief excerpts from the *Big Book of Alcoholics Anonymous* and *Twelve Steps and Twelve Traditions* are reprinted with permission of Alcoholics Anonymous World Services, Inc. (AAWS). Permission to reprint these excerpts does not mean that AAWS has reviewed or approved the contents of this publication, or that AAWS necessarily agrees with the views expressed herein. AA is a program of recovery from alcoholism only; use of these excerpts in connection with programs and activities that are patterned after AA but address other problems, or in any other non-AA context, do not imply otherwise. Additionally, while AA is a spiritual program, AA is not a religious program. Thus, AA is not affiliated or allied with any sect, denomination, or specific religious belief.

The Mother Teresa Center. *Mother Teresa: Come Be My Light; The Private Writings of the Saint of Calcutta.* The Mother Teresa Center, exclusive licensee throughout the world of the Missionaries of Charity for the works of Mother Teresa. Used with permission.

T. S. Eliot. Four Quartets: The Little Gidding, Houghton Mifflin Harcourt. Used with permission.

T. S. Eliot. *Little Gidding (Four Quartets)* and *The Love Song of J. Alfred Prufrock.* Used with permission from Faber and Faber Publishers.

Warren W. Wiersbe. Excerpted from *Pray, Praise, and Promises.* Used with permission.

Webster's New World College Dictionary, 3rd Edition. Used by permission from Cengage Learning.

ABOUT THE AUTHOR

Rev. Dr. Jim Stout is an ordained Presbyterian minister who has pastored in five churches. His other ministry experiences include working with college and graduate students at` Harvard, MIT, Boston, Northeastern, and Miami universities; doing social work with Young Life's outreach to teenage gangs in New York City; and working as student chaplain to  the men's violent ward at Danvers Massachusetts State Mental Hospital.

He was given the National Alliance for the Mentally Ill (NAMI) California's "Distinguished Clergy Award" for his efforts on behalf of those affected by mental illness.

In college, he participated in varsity football and wrestling, and won Golden Gloves heavyweight boxing championships in Pennsylvania and Ohio. Since then, he has competed in triathlons and finished seven- and eight-day group rides on his bike.

He received his Master of Divinity from Gordon-Conwell Theological Seminary and his Doctor of Ministry from Fuller Theological Seminary.

He has been married to the former Leah Ann Hayden since 1967. They have two sons, Jim Jr. and John, and four energetic grandchildren.

THANKS FOR READING!

If this book has been helpful to you, please give it a review and share it with others. A quick, honest review on Amazon (it takes less than a minute) will help others discover the book. I'd love to hear your stories of how this book has helped you, and your feedback will help me improve this book and many future writing projects.

Consider gifting copies to people who might also benefit. But first, please listen carefully to their pain and add your own supportive words of strength, hope, and experience.

Would you like to schedule an interview or speaking engagement? Please contact me through my website at www.drjimstout.com. Unfortunately, my schedule does not permit personal counseling.

Want to stay up-to-date with my new books and articles? Please join my newsletter for great articles and behind-the-scenes looks at upcoming books.

You'll also reveive a FREE digital copy of my book *Recovering and Rebuilding from a Severe Mental Illness*, which shares my personal story of faith and reveals how I recovered from crippling depression and bipolar disorder. It will also equip you with the tools you need to overcome the damaging effects of mental illness in your own life.

To join, please visit www.drjimstout.com/join.

Made in the USA
Charleston, SC
23 May 2016